# WEAPONS OF OUR WARFARE

Now is the Time for the Church to Go on the Offense

T. Jerry Caver

Weapons of Our Warfare Copyright © 2019 by Dr. T Jerry Caver. All Rights Reserved.

All rights reserved. No part of this book may be reproduced in any form or by any electronic or mechanical means including information storage and retrieval systems, without permission in writing from the author. The only exception is by a reviewer, who may quote short excerpts in a review.

This book and cover, was designed and prepared to be published by Tracey Kummrow at TNT Xpressions. tntxpressions@cox.net

Dr. T. Jerry Caver

Printed in the United States of America

ISBN- 9781797743288

*This book is dedicated to My Father-God who loves me enough to put up with my hard head and tender heart, who in His love, sent Jesus to die for all my sins, of which there were many. The One who called me to a closer walk with him and used someone who was unqualified, to bring Him glory.*

# ACKNOWLEDGMENT

Today I would like to give credit to those men who had such an influence on my life:

Kenneth Hagen, for teaching me about faith and the Baptism of the Holy Spirit. Kenneth Copeland, who taught me how-to walk-in faith. Bill Dearman, who was my spiritual father. John Osteen, who spoke the truth of the Gospel to me and prayed for me when I had cancer. Carl Lupenitz, who taught me how to hear from God and how to be an effective missionary, with signs and wonders in our ministry. I would not be the man of God I am today without the influence of these men in my life. It is my prayer that I can be this type of influence to other young men starting out in the ministry that these men were to me.

Dr. T. Jerry Caver – Dean of Citadel Bible College

# CONTENTS

## WEAPONS OF OUR WARFARE

### Now is the Time for the Church to Go on the Offense

| | | |
|---|---|---|
| INTRODUCTION | | 5 |
| CHAPTER 1 | WEAPONS OF OUR WARFARE | 11 |
| CHAPTER 2 | DAILY CONFESSIONS | 25 |
| CHAPTER 3 | SWORD OF THE SPIRIT -WORD OF GOD | 31 |
| CHAPTER 4 | PRAYER AS A WEAPON | 37 |
| CHAPTER 5 | ALL KINDS OF PRAYER | 55 |
| CHAPTER 6 | THE NAME OF JESUS | 73 |
| CHAPTER 7 | TONGUES | 109 |
| CHAPTER 8 | HIGH PRAISE | 115 |
| CHAPTER 9 | A SHOUT OF VICTORY | 119 |
| CHAPTER 10 | PROPHETIC DECREES | 121 |
| ABOUT THE AUTHOR | | 127 |

Dr. T. Jerry Caver

# INTRODUCTION

The reason for this book is that I was thinking about what it would take for the Church today to be the Church without spot and wrinkle. We are not that victorious Church that we read about in the Bible. Knowing the time, we are in, which I believe is the "End Times," the Church should have more influence on world events than we do. All my life, I have been looking forward to the "great end-time revival," where the Church will see a great influx of people getting saved and delivered. We are not seeing that in the church today.

The question I asked myself was "why?" I believe God has given us the weapons to be that overcoming, victorious, church that we read about in the Bible. Either, the church does not know these weapons or has not been taught about them. I am a firm believer that if we repeat what the first church did, we will have the same results as they did. From my almost 80 years of life, and 60 years of experience in the ministry, I believe I have gained some knowledge that needs to be shared with others so that they could learn from my experiences.

This book is to educate those who want to live an overcoming, victorious life for Christ who gave His all, to provide us with the weapons of our warfare to defeat the devil and his group of demons. Most Of those who call themselves Christians don't study the Bible to find these things out for themselves. If they knew the gifts that God gave us to be victorious, they would do what the Bible tells them to do. In other words, they are hearers of the Word, but not doers of that Word. Jesus is coming soon, and He is coming back for a victorious, overcoming church without spot or wrinkle.

Everyone has the opportunity to hear. There is a church on every corner, and the Gospel is preached on the radio, and television. We have no excuses here. It is the choices we have made that will condemn us to Hell or have eternal life in heaven with Jesus. Either way we will have eternal life, but it matters where we will spend it.

The scripture in John 15:14 that frightens me is where Jesus said, *"You are my friend if you do my commandments."* Notice he didn't say "if they say the sinner's prayer" or make a decision, or go to church regularly or even teach a Sunday school class. No! He said, "Obey my commandments." As a Christian, you can't do His commandments if you don't study His word to see what the commandments are. You may explore the Bible and say that commandment is not for today. Jesus is the same yesterday, today and forever and if Jesus is the same, His commandments are the same.

God never changes, and His Word has never changed regardless of what some denominations say. My Father has it all planned out. He is a miracle working God who still wants to do them today and He does for those who believe God's Word. He has given us the power to be witnesses and to be victorious in every

area of our life, but yet the church is losing ground to the devil and his crew every year.

I had a Pastor friend who said, "If the Bible says a rooster can pull a freight train, your response should be, hook him up." That is how you are to read the Bible. It means what it says, and says what it means. We read and learn that we are healed and we say we believe the Bible as the Word of God; but wallow around in our sickness, see the best human physicians and specialists and finally when they can't get us well we turn to the Lord. You haven't been building your faith up by believing God for your headache, and now you are trying to build your faith by believing that God will heal you from some fatal disease. It won't happen for most Christians; most will die in their sickness because of little faith. Usually, God gets a bad name for not healing that person. It is not God's fault; it is ours for not having our faith built up. Without Faith, it is impossible to please God, or without faith, it is impossible to receive your healing.

Learn and use your weapons of this spiritual warfare and you can be more than a conqueror and be victorious, and an overcoming Christian. Jesus called us more than conquerors. How are we more than conquerors?

Let me give you this example: This man is a prizefighter, he trains and trains for a fight. As we watch the fight, we see that it is a close fight; each prizefighter keeps hitting the opponent with hard blows with their fists. It is a long and fierce battle. Both are bruised and bloody, finally, one gets the deciding blow and knocks his opponent out. They give him the prize money. He is the conqueror. He goes home and walks through the door of his house and his wife holds out her hands, and he gives her the prize money. She is more than a conqueror. Her husband paid the price to become the champion and then gave all the rewards to her the same way Jesus did for us and we became more than conquerors. Jesus paid the price for us on the cross. He was raised from the dead by the Holy Spirit. He beat Satan to a pulp and dragged Him through the streets of Hell and He preached to the saints in Abraham's bosom; and then Jesus and the saints ascended to Father-God in heaven. Jesus was victorious over death, Hell and the grave. The Bible says He then gave gifts to the church; a victory over the devil where Jesus took back from Satan, the things he got from Adam. Jesus gave back to the church, dominion over the world, eternal life, and He reinstated us so we could have fellowship with Father-God again. Being more than a conqueror is great! Now we have to learn how to use the weapons that Jesus gave us to be more than a conqueror!

## CHAPTER ONE

# "WEAPONS OF OUR WARFARE"

One of the first things anyone in the military learns is the weapons he will use to defeat the enemy. The military members must know their weaponry forward and backward, and how to clean, take apart, and assemble them blindfolded. I am afraid that is not so with Christians. We try to go into spiritual battles with one or two weapons that we have been trained with when the task may take our entire arsenal to defeat the enemy. Sometimes, it takes only one to do the job. What if we left our weapon at home, forgot it, didn't know how to use it, or we didn't know we had it, like some Christians? The battle takes much longer to win, and you might take more casualties than if you had the right weapon or weapons.

## NOW IS THE TIME FOR BELIEVERS TO GO ON THE OFFENSE

The world looks at the church as a bunch of losers; poorly misguided hypocrites, who say they are victorious but look nothing like they say. We Christians should be ashamed to let the devil, and his demons run over us and then ask God for forgiveness for not receiving the benefits that Jesus paid for on the cross. How many of us believe the church should be victorious and overcome evil with good? But most of the church, "in general" is a defeated foe of the devil, which talks the talk but doesn't walk the walk. They walk around looking like they have been sucking on lemons and wonder why no one wants to come to their church. We are not even winning enough souls to keep up with the death rate of our older Christians. Do you know why? People don't want what we have because they already have as much, and sure don't want more of the same. Most of the churchgoers live the same way as non-Christians do. They have the same poverty, the same health concerns, and the same divorce rate. Most have the same problems. These types of church members have no effect on their community or the world around them, much less in their own lives. What does your life look like? Does the non-Christian recognize that you are a Christian by the way you live your life and how you speak? A non-Christian can't see spiritual things, so in order for them to see and want what we have, they must see physical things. Such as, does the Christian have a good family life? Do they keep their house and yard in order? Do the children listen to their parents? Does a non-Christian see the love of Christ in your actions towards the school, police, or even in the restaurants when dealing with the waitress?

They see how you treat other people, friends, and non-friends. We should notice our actions so others say, "Boy that guy has something going and I wish I had it." Do we want them to see that there is something different about us and then desire what we have? Yes, we do. In most cases they see nothing, and that is not God's plan for us! He expects the world to see something in you that they are missing in their own life.

2nd Corinthians 10: 3-5, *"for though we walk in the flesh. WE DO NOT WAR according to the flesh. For the WEAPONS of our warfare are not carnal but Mighty in God for the pulling down strongholds, casting down arguments and every high thing that exalts itself against the knowledge of God, bringing every thought into captivity to the obedience of Christ."*

If you have more weapons than your enemy, it makes it easier for you to win the battle. For example; if you have ten tanks, and your enemy has one tank, which one will win the battle?

## POWER FACTOR EQUATION

Deuteronomy 32:29-30a

*Oh, that they were wise that they understood this: that they would consider their latter end. How could one chase a thousand and two put ten thousand to flight...*

## Notice this Power Factor, Equation:

| | A name 1 person = 1000 to flee | | |
|---|---|---|---|
| | 2 persons = 10,000 to flee | | |
| **Multiplication Equation of Times Ten** | | | |
| **Persons** | | **X 10** | **To Flee** |
| 3 persons = | 10,000 | X 10 | 100,000<br>1 Hundred Thousand |
| 4 persons = | 100,000 | X 10 | 1,000,000<br>1 million |
| 5 persons = | 1,000,000 | X 10 | 10,000,000<br>10 million |
| 6 persons = | 10,000,000 | X 10 | 100,000,000<br>100 million |
| 7 persons = | 100,000,000 | X 10 | 1,000,000,000<br>1 billion |
| 8 persons = | 1,000,000,000 | X 10 | 10,000,000,000<br>10 billion |
| 9 persons = | 10,000,000,000 | X 10 | 100,000,000,000<br>100 billion |
| 10 persons = | 100,000,000,000 | X 10 | 1,000,000,000,000<br>1 trillion |
| 100 persons = | 1, and (303) zeros. | | |
| My computer calculates this figure, and I don't know if there is a name for that many zeros. | | | |

This is how much power we generate when we are in unity and are saying the same thing.

Christian weapons are powerful and are awesome when you use them and power is multiplied because of the power factor equation.

Let's talk about the "Weapons" that Paul was talking about in this scripture.

## ARMOR OF GOD

In the military, when you are going into battle, they issued each man a bullet-proof vest. That is for your defense. Jesus gave us the Armor of God, for our defense. We need to put it on and keep it on, so the devil can't sneak up on you and hit you with something you don't want.

Turn to Ephesians 6: 11-18,

*Put on the whole armor of God that you may be able to stand against the <u>wiles</u> of the devil. $^{12}$ For we do not wrestle against flesh and blood, but against principalities, against powers, against the rulers of the darkness of this age, against spiritual hosts of wickedness in the heavenly places. $^{13}$ Therefore take up the whole armor of God that you may be able to withstand in the evil day, and having done all, to stand. $^{14}$ Stand therefore, having girded your waist with truth,* *having put on the breastplate of righteousness, <sup>15</sup> and having shod your feet with the preparation of the gospel of peace; <sup>16</sup> above all, taking the shield of faith with which you will be able to quench all the fiery darts of the wicked one. <sup>17</sup> And take the helmet of salvation, and the sword of the Spirit, which is the word of God; <sup>18</sup> praying always with all prayer and supplication in the Spirit, being watchful to this end with all perseverance and supplication for all the saints—*

The devils "Wiles" are his tricks and strategies to defeat you. If you notice, all this armor is to protect the front of the saint. There is no armor for the back, which implies we should always be alert and stand to face the enemy. The reason Paul was using this example, was that they chained him to a Roman soldier, and he was a visible example used.

After some studying about the Roman armor; I found things that were very interesting. First, the shields they used could be hooked together at the bottom and fit on both sides, so they made a solid defense all across the ranks. The soldiers were in ranks of one hundred, ten men across, and ten men deep. One requirement the men in the back ranks had, was to push the man in front of him. They pushed the enemy over and walked on them. The interesting detail about walking on them was the shoes they wore. The shoes they wore in battle had three-inch spikes, unlike the spiked heels women wear today, but similar to football cleats. The three-inch steel spikes were small enough to go through the chainmail armor the enemy would wear. When the Roman soldiers walked on the enemy, the spikes of ten men would kill them. The shoes worn when the soldiers were not in battle, had less than one-inch spikes for keeping the peace. Can you imagine when the Romans were in crowd control and then stepped on your sandaled feet? This adds a new meaning to "shod" your feet with the gospel of peace, doesn't it? The Roman soldier carried two swords into battle. A short one for fighting with the shield and a long one for fighting without. The soldier fighting with a shield could pivot it and create an opening, so he could thrust the short sword through without exposing himself to the enemy. The fighting block formation was effective because they hooked their shields entirely around the formation to cover them, in case, the enemy surrounded them.

## EPHESIANS 6: 11-18

These scriptures tell us who we are, who we are to be fighting against, and what we must do so we will be victorious in this battle. It is simple, put on the armor of God. Who do you look like when you put on the armor of God? You look like God. The devil doesn't know it's not God until we speak. Then, for some of us, our confession gives the devil all the ammunition he needs to keep us defeated.

1. We don't confess what God says about us.

2. Many Christians confess what the devil has been telling them.

3. We don't believe God's Word even if we profess that we do.

4. We confess what the Dr. says about us. Remember, doctors, are only practicing and are not the final authority.

There are many things we confess and don't even realize we are charting a course we don't want to go because of the things we say. Watch your mouth! Think of what you will say before you spout off. The greatest weapons of our warfare are the words spoken out of our mouth. Our mouth is the greatest weapon when we confess the Word of God and say what God says. Somehow, we think if we keep confessing the Word that something will happen. Sorry, but there is no faith in that method. It takes believing what you are confessing. Confession has a big part to play in our walk with Jesus, and it starts at the beginning when we were first saved.

Romans 10:9-10, *"that if you confess with your mouth the Lord Jesus and believe in your heart that God raised Him from the dead, you will be saved. (10) For with the heart one believes unto righteousness, and with the mouth, confession is made unto salvation."* Without our confession, it would be hard to be saved. Confessing our sins gets us forgiveness when we ask, and forgiveness makes us clean again. What we say with our mouths, our confession has much to do with our Christian walk.

1st Timothy 6:12 states, *"Fight the good fight of Faith, lay hold on eternal life, to which you were also called and have confessed the good confession in the presence of many witnesses."* Another Scripture, Hebrews 10:10, *"Let us hold fast to our confession of our hope without wavering for He who promised is faithful."* The "without wavering" is what gets most Christians.

We see in these two scriptures that our confession has something to do with our Faith and Hope. Let's talk about Faith first. How do you get faith? The Bible says, *"So then, Faith comes by hearing and hearing by the Word of God."* Hebrews 10:17. Notice, it says hearing and hearing, I like to say "Faith comes by me saying and hearing and saying and hearing until Faith comes." Sometimes, I have to confess and hear the scripture one hundred times or more before the faith comes. At that point, I know that I know the promise is mine. It is the same; as "I know that I know" when you have that knowledge of being saved. You know without a shadow of a doubt you are and no one could convince you that you are not saved. You just know it. You have that same knowledge when faith drops into your heart about any scripture. Faith is always NOW or as the Bible says, Now Faith is...

## HOPE

Hope is that expectation you get from Faith. Hope in Hebrews 11:1 is not wishing as it is used in our everyday language; Such as "I hope so." In this context of hope, we are wishing it might happen. In Hebrews 11:1, we see a holy expectation. *"Now faith is the substance of things hoped for, the evidence of things not seen."* The NIV gives us a little better understanding of this verse, Hebrews 11:1, *"Now faith is (our full) confidence in what we hope for and assurance about what we do not see."*

Here is another explanation from Matthew Henry Commentaries.

What Hope is:

"It is a firm persuasion and expectation, that God will perform all he has promised to us in Christ. This persuasion gives the soul to enjoy those things now; it gives them a subsistence or reality in the soul, by the first-fruits and foretastes of them. Faith proves to the mind, the reality of things that cannot be seen by the bodily eye. It is full approval of all God has revealed, as holy, just, and good."

It is by our confession and our hearing that Faith comes. If I confess I am healed for a while and I am still sick, does that make the Bible a lie where it is written: *By the stripes, on Jesus back you are healed?*" Isaiah 53:5. No, we should continue to confess our healing.

What happens when we start agreeing with the doctor? "I got so and so" This is a negative confession and if we confess it a long time, it becomes closer to reality and soon we will have it. We need to confess the scriptures. When I had cancer, I confessed two pages of scriptures daily to receive my healing. I would listen to the healing scriptures at night with earphones all night long. I wasn't healed supernaturally, but I heard God's plan through my time in prayer. He said to have surgery, but don't take chemo or radiation. My doctor insisted I take them, but I told him, "No, God said not to receive them." I have been cancer free for 24 years at this writing. Was I healed, Yes? Was it the way I expected it? No. But I am healed. To maintain my healing, I confess this scripture to this day. Nahum 1:9 KJV. *The Lord will make an utter end of it. Affliction will not rise up a second time.* I know that I know that it will not come back. I have to confess, so my foolish mind won't receive the devil's thoughts and that it will bring my thoughts back into captivity to the truth I am healed. This is not the "Name it and Claim it," type of confession. That type is "mind over matter," if I don't mind, it won't matter. You cannot stand in the garage and confess that you are a car and suddenly become a

Mercedes. You can't confess you are rich without obeying what the Bible tells you about your money so you will become rich.

Your confession is based on the Word of God. Find scriptures that pertain to the problem and be a doer of the Word and confess God's promises until faith drops into your heart, and you have what you say.

According to Mark 11:22-24, *"So Jesus answered and said to them, Have faith in God. 23 For assuredly, I say to you, whoever says to this mountain, 'Be removed and be cast into the sea,' and does not doubt in his heart, but believes that those things he says will be done, he will have whatever he says. 24 Therefore I say to you, whatever things you ask when you pray, believe that you receive them, and you will have them."* We can confess that we believe the scriptures, and we may believe them in our mind, but it is not until you believe them in your heart, that the problem is removed. That is what confession does. It causes you to get past the mind into the heart where you know that you know it is yours.

CHAPTER TWO

# "DAILY CONFESSIONS"

Here are some confessions I have said for years. I don't even know if I wrote them or someone else wrote them, but I have confessed them since I can remember. In the blanks, you can add my wife, my family, or my Church.

For with my mouth confession is made unto salvation. Romans 10:9-10

When (My) _____ and I can call upon the Lord and He will answer us. Jeremiah 33:3

No weapon formed against me or (my) _____ shall prosper. Isaiah 54:17, but whatever (my) _____ and I do, it shall prosper. Psalms 1:3

Greater is He that is in me and (my) _____ that he that is in the world. 1st John 4:4

The Lord has given His angels charge over me and my _____ and they will keep us in all our ways. Proverbs 12:28.

(My) _____ and I are doers of the Word, not hearers only. James 1:22, No evil will befall me and (my) _____; neither shall any plague come to our house. Psalms 91:10-11

Christ has redeemed me and (my) _____ from the curse of the Law. Galatians 3:13-14

Therefore, I forbid any sickness or disease to come upon this body or on my spouse or on my children. Every disease, germ and every virus that touches our bodies shall die instantly in the Name of Jesus.

(My) _____ and I delight ourselves in the Lord and He gives us the desires of our heart. Psalms 37:4, *We have given and it is given unto us, good measure, pressed down, and shaken together, running over shall be given unto our bosom.* Luke 6:38, *With what measure we give, it shall be given unto us. We have sown bountifully; therefore, we shall reap bountifully.* 2nd Corinthians 9:6-8, *Our family has no lack, for my God supplies all our needs according to His riches in Glory by Christ Jesus.* Philippians 4:19.

The Lord is our shepherd and WE DO NOT WANT. Psalms 23:1 Jesus came that (my) _____ and I might have life, and have it more abundantly. John 10:10.

(My) _____ and I have received the gift of righteousness and reign in life as Kings by Christ Jesus. Romans 5:17. The Spirit of truth lives in me and (my) _____ and teaches us all things and guides us into all truths.

Therefore, I confess I have perfect knowledge of every situation and every circumstance that we come up against. For we have the wisdom of God. John 16:13, James 1:5. Jesus is made unto (my) _____ and I, wisdom, righteousness, sanctification, and redemption.

Therefore, we confess we have the wisdom of God and we are the righteousness of God in Jesus Christ. 1st Corinthians 1:30, 2nd Corinthians 5:21.

(My) _____ and I are new creations in Christ: we are His workmanship created in Christ Jesus.

Therefore, we have the mind of Christ and His wisdom is formed within us.

We have a sound mind and our memory is blessed. 2nd Corinthians 5:17, Ephesians 2:10, 1st Corinthians 2:16, Psalms 10:7, 2nd Timothy 1:7

(My) _____ and I am increasing in the knowledge of God. We are strengthened with all might according to His Glorious power. Colossians 1:10-11

(My) _____ and I are born of God and we have world overcoming faith residing on the inside of us. For greater is He that is in us, than he that is in the world. 1st John 5:4-5, 1st John 4:4

(My) _____ and I will let no corrupt communication proceed out of our mouth because *our mouth is the well of life.* Ephesians 4:29, Psalms 10:1

(My) _____ and I will not let the Word of God depart from before our eyes for it is the LIFE to us, for we have found in it, is health and healing to all our flesh. Prov. 4:21-22 Jesus gave (my) _____ and I, the authority to use His name, and that which we bind on earth is bound in heaven. And what we loose on earth is loosed in heaven.

Therefore, in the Name of Jesus Christ, we bind the principalities, the powers, the rulers of the darkness of this world. We bind and cast down spiritual wickedness in high places and render them harmless and ineffective against me, (my) _____ and my church. I, therefore, loose the Holy Spirit and the angels assigned to me to cause the good things spoken by God the Father in His Word to become a reality in our life. Ephesians 6:12, Matthew 16:19, John 16:23-24

And this is the confidence that we have in Jesus, that if we ask ANYTHING according to His will, His Word, He hears us, and if we know that He hears us, *WHATSOEVER WE ASK WE KNOW THAT WE HAVE THE PETITIONS that we desired of Him.* 1st John 5:14-15

To be healed, we must believe we ARE healed. To be victorious, we must believe we ARE victorious. To be prosperous? We must first do what the Bible tells us to do with our money, tithe, and offerings, and then believe in our prosperity. We must have faith in God's word. Where is your faith level? You don't have to tell anyone where it is. The life you are living tells on you and is a billboard that everyone reads including the lost.

CHAPTER THREE

# THE FIRST WEAPON
# THE SWORD OF THE SPIRIT
# THE WORD OF GOD

The only weapon of offense mentioned in Ephesians 6:17, *17 "And take the helmet of salvation, and the sword of the Spirit, which is the word of God."* How did Jesus overcome the temptations in the wilderness? He quoted the scriptures (the Word of God) to the devil. He is using the Sword of the Spirit to defeat the devil. Here, again, this involves your mouth. Remembering, it was by God's mouth and His words, that the world was created. By speaking His words in faith, we create our world and defeat the devil.

We have an arsenal of weapons that God has given us, but most of us can't name any besides maybe prayer and the sword of the Spirit. Before you can use your sword and quote scriptures, you must know some scriptures. How often do you study the Bible? I didn't say to read the Bible; I said study it. Reading the Bible is good, but studying the Bible is best.

Revelation 1:16: *"He had in His right hand seven stars, out of His mouth went a sharp two-edged sword,*

In this scripture, we see Jesus will destroy the evil in this world "with the two-edged sword, His mouth speaking the Word of God" It is interesting to me that all the evidence of our victory in this life hinges on what we say. Since we are made in His image, He demonstrates in His Word, how we are to obtain victory in this life.

Here is another interesting scripture. Revelation 19: 13-15, *He was clothed with a robe dipped in blood, and His name is called The Word of God. 14 And the armies in heaven, clothed in fine linen, white and clean, followed Him on white horses. 15 Now out of His mouth goes a sharp sword, that with it He should strike the nations. And He Himself will rule them with a rod of iron. He Himself treads the winepress of the fierceness and wrath of Almighty God.*

The church needs to get ready to go horseback riding, and I hope you like white horses. We see in this scripture that Jesus whose name is "The Word of God" will have a sharp sword coming out of His mouth to strike the nations. It's my opinion that we, the armies of God in the heavens, will go into battle. I think it will be an all God thing pertaining to the battle. We will only observe Jesus strike the nations. I don't see us, the church, using any weapons. I have read books and opinions. Some say we will use the weapon of our warfare to battle with Jesus.

This is for free and only my opinion, but I don't believe that Jesus will need our help. Don't count my statement as the Word of God or thus says the Lord. You need to have your own opinion by studying the Word of God and reading other views. Opinions are just that. You and I can have opposite ones and still fellowship and love one another. We will probably find out that both of us are wrong when we get to heaven. That is some of the trouble with the church today. We are too dogmatic about our views and break fellowship with one another because we have a different interpretation of the Word of God. There are a few things that we could break fellowship over, and the most important one of them is "there is only one way to salvation." Anything that is of a different belief and doesn't state that Jesus is the only way, you should not fellowship with them. Some of their wrong belief might rub off on you.

*John :9-11, Whoever transgresses and does not abide in the doctrine of Christ does not have God. He who abides in the doctrine of Christ has both the Father and the Son. 10 If anyone comes to you and does not bring this doctrine, do not receive him into your house nor greet him; 11 for he who greets him shares in his evil deeds.*

Here again, is my opinion: If they believe that Jesus was born of a virgin, crucified on a cross for our sin, and He rose from the dead and is at the right hand of the Father, then I should be able to fellowship with them. It is because of petty differences that the Body of Christ is not in unity. Therefore, the devil is causing so much trouble in our church and our country. We must pursue a body of Christ that believes nearest to what we believe and join that Pastor's vision. If it's not your vision, you need to keep looking. But that should not keep us from fellowship. Many churches have split over petty differences. People want their own way and form an almost hatred for the other group. I have my opinion of what the Bible says, and you have yours. If the truth were known, it would be very hard to find many that have exact beliefs. My Pastors, whom I love, and respect, don't believe 100% how I do, and that is OK. It doesn't mean we have to break fellowship with one another. My God told me to hook up with their vision to see it completed. That I will do. I will be loyal, faithful, dependable, and love them with all my heart. I will overlook anything that I think they have missed or disagree with.

It is God's job to correct and change the course of that body, not mine or your job. Our job is to pray for the Pastors. It is not our job to criticize the Pastor or their direction they are taking in the church. If you want to be blessed, hook up with their vision. If you want the devil having a free run at you, just start talking to other people about disagreements you have with the Pastor. God will remove His hand of protection over you. You are in a very dangerous place.

CHAPTER FOUR

# PRAYER AS A WEAPON

First, we must know what prayer is before we can use it as a weapon. Prayer is our needs crying out for help. Many Christians say we are not to pray for our needs because God already knows them, but it is alright to thank Him for supplying them. Prayer is born when there is a need. Some people pray in hoping, wishing and begging. This type of prayer comes from people who do not have a relationship with our heavenly Father. They may be Christians, know Jesus as their Savior, and may love Him with all their heart, but they don't have an intimacy with the Father. John 16:23, This scripture tells us to ask the Father, not Jesus for our needs. Those that have a relationship with the Father pray differently than those that don't have a relationship. They pray in faith because they have the assurance that their need will be met. Brother E.W. Kenyon said it like this "Prayer is the Living Word in

Lips of Faith," Prayer is like a mirror. You hold His Word up to God, and He sees Himself in the Word. All our needs are covered by the Word of God. Somewhere in the Bible, God has said he would meet that need. You find it and you have His promise He will do it. When we are speaking His Words back to Him, we are holding up the collateral he gave us (like a bank would hold collateral for a loan); that He would do His Word. Prayer is facing God with man's needs and His promise to meet those needs.

Jesus taught us to pray. He taught us to trust Him and His Word. Jesus and the Father are one. John 1:1, Jesus was the Father's Word sent to earth so mankind could have sense knowledge of His Word. It is only through studying the Bible that we can know the Father. Through revelation knowledge, we receive from the Holy Spirit living in us. The Father is a Spirit and the only way we can know Him is by the Spirit. When we ask Jesus to be our Lord, the Holy Spirit comes and lives in us. He tells us what the Father's thoughts are, and revelation knowledge. Prayer is a vital part of our relationship with the Father. Jesus taught us to pray and to trust His Word. God encourages us to act on

His Word. It is in this prayer that we can have a relationship with the Father.

Luke 18:1 Jesus said, *"Then He spoke a parable to them, that men always ought to pray and not lose heart."* How long is "always?" There are two ways to say that scripture in today's English. Brother Kenyon quoted it this way. "Men ought always to pray and not turn out badly." Or "Men ought always to pray and not cave in" In prayer, we can get so near the Father that you can breathe in His presence.

Prayer gives us the right to boldly come into the Throne room and be in His presence. Remember the story about the woman with the issue of blood, who touched Jesus and was healed. I was reading in a Bible that had multi-translations. One of the translations said *"Jesus said someone touched me" and the disciples said "Master, the multitudes press you and crush you," but He answered, "No, someone has made a demand on my ability."* Prayer is making a demand on God's ability to meet the need.

## PRAYER IS A SPIRITUAL EXERCISE

In prayer, your spirit is contacting the Father. Paul said, "My spirit and the Lord Jesus will be with you in your deliberations. That doesn't sound possible to the natural man. Our sense knowledge can't grasp this; only in the realm of the recreated spirit, we can understand it. We become ONE with Him. We are no longer interested in me, myself, and mine. When we are One with God, we only have One agenda. We become so ruled by the Word and the Holy Spirit, we become masters of those demons that always seem to cause problems in our life. We cast out demons with the Word, instead of speaking the problems that always happen. When we do that, we are having more faith in the problem's source, then what the Word says about the problem.

Our weakness is destroyed by the strengths of God when we become ONE with Him. When we are one with God, the Word becomes the sword of the spirit and it is waging a war against demonic forces. His Word through your lips dominates the forces of evil. Jesus said, "In my name, you shall cast out demons." This means, you rule them, and govern them. God through you can sway nations. Now, you can understand 2nd Corinthians 6:1 *"Laboring together with Him."* How? It is through this marvelous prayer life. When you become one with Him, you have entered the Holy Priesthood in your life. You can be God's voice, His spokesman, His ambassador, His under-ruler in Jesus name with His Words on your lips. You are taking Jesus' place in this world. You will act in His place. We are His body here on earth. You remember that God gave Adam dominion over the entire universe. That dominion was restored to us through Jesus, but it is no value to us unless we use the authority in His Name. That authority was given to Adam is now given to us as believers in the Name. Jesus exercised that dominion. He ruled the sea, the fishes, and He ruled the human body. He also fed the multitudes. Jesus did not exercise any authority that is not still available for us today.

Someday, there will be people raised up that will take the Name of Jesus. They will bless humanity as Jesus did. Do you want to be one of those? I do. The secret to it is to be ONE with God. Are you willing to pay the price? Or do you just want to be the happy defeated Christian you are today? Did Jesus not say in Matthew 28:18-20, *And Jesus came and spoke to them, saying,*

*"All authority has been given to Me in heaven and on earth. 19 Go therefore and make disciples of all the nations, baptizing them in the name of the Father and of the Son and of the Holy Spirit, 20 teaching them to observe all things that I have commanded you; and lo, I am with you always, even to the end of the age."* Amen. He is with us in the Word, in His Name, and He is with us in the presence of the Holy Spirit. We can join forces with Him by having a prayer life. All the authority that is in His name is in our lips. We need to let that authority loose. We can give it liberty and bless men. He made us sons, and He has given us His Name. He has given us the Holy Spirit and has restored all that Adam lost and more. We are Satan's rulers. Why did He redeem us? Why make us a New Creation and why make us righteous?

Why dwell in us? Why give us the Name? So, we will be, good neutral sons and daughters, who never face the enemy; who simply read the Word but never act on it? Is God still living, and are we tied up with Him? God's question to us today is, "Are you as serious about oneness with me as you are about feeding your belly?" Are you as serious about promoting Jesus as you are about promoting your ministry? Are my

Redemption and New Creation as real as taxes? Does it mean anything? We must face the issue. We are surrounded by demonic forces that are dominating the humans on earth, and we have the authority over them. Why are these forces still doing their evil? Our prayer is the method and mode for dominating these demonic powers that are wrecking our civilization.

## TAKING OUR PLACE

Everyone has a place in prayer life. God has no unused members, just as there are no parts of your body that are not used. It is the same way in the Spiritual body of Christ. From the moment you are born into the body of Christ, you have a place to work. You don't have to have training, only be born-again. Too many members have been listening to the devil, and he tells them they don't have a place. You have a place! In some churches, there are those that think they have the job to criticize others in the church because they want them to do more. Criticizing is not one position or job in the church. Nor is it one of the gifts the Holy Spirit gives out. Your business is to find your place and fill it. Take your place! Spend time in prayer, studying the Bible and meditating on that

Word. Don't allow anything to stand in your way of finding your place. Some might say, "I haven't been called to a life of prayer. "No, but we are called to have a relationship with Father-God, and there are only two ways to have a relationship with Him.

Luke 18:1: *"through prayer and the word."* There is a need for us all to pray for the salvation of others. That is part of our job description. There will be those whose blood will be on us if we do not pray for the lost. If you see those in your church going through problems and you don't pray for them and they fall away, it is your fault you did not pray. God, have mercy on us because we are too occupied with our pleasures, dreams, and plans that we did not pray for our brothers and sisters and the enemy captured them. If you are upset about crime, and lawlessness from the youth of this generation, and disturbed about their permissive sex outlook on life; this has happened because parents were too occupied with their own pleasures and work, to give love and discipline to their children. We no longer have the privilege to pray; it's no longer a privilege; it's our duty, or the blood of our children that go to Hell, will be on our heads. May God have mercy on the man or woman that will have to stand and explain to God why their child went to Hell. There are many children that grow up in Christian homes but do not have the restraining power of God over their lives. These children don't want to go to church, and the parents let them stay at home I have seen parents put school work ahead of being in God's presence. That shows the child, how important the church is to the parent. Rebellious children don't want to do anything that the parents want, and the parents don't make them. You want a pleasant, happy life when your children become teens, spank and discipline them when they are small. Don't let the child tell you what to do. You tell them what to do. The restraining power of God comes from being disciplined by the parents. Never in the age of man has the youth been as uncontrollable as they are now. The reason is apparent! The mothers and fathers have failed in their responsibilities to the children and to God. We are the reason for all the crime and lawlessness in this country. What are we going to do about it? We better stay on our knees and pray until God can bring a change. Take up your responsibilities, Now!

## IN HIS PRESENCE

In the beginning, in the Garden of Eden, Adam lived in the presence of God, and like a child, he would crawl up into his father's arms. Adam made a big mistake by selling his great and wonderful privileges to the enemy. Then the presence of God was taken away from him. God sent an angel with a flaming sword at the gate of the garden to keep Adam and Eve out of God's presence. Think, of all the years that the two of them could look over at the garden, longing to be in God's presence again. The Garden of Eden was known and looked upon for thousands of years; possibly until the flood came and destroyed everything. Adam lived for 930 years, and I'm sure, not one day passed where he didn't wish he was back in God's presence. Many years after the flood, God cut a covenant with another man, Abraham. God said through his bloodline, the Messiah would come and bring back the presence of God. The Children of Israel experienced God's presence in the Holy of Holies, but could not approach it without sacrifice. The Priest had to be covered with the smoke of incense, because of being a sinner, and if he looked at the Glory of God, it would kill him. God was still unapproachable in the Holy of Holies. Later, Jesus said in John 14:6 *"I am the way, the truth, and the life."*

These are the names of the three doors in the tabernacle.

1. "The Life" is the name of the only door in the wall of curtains around the tabernacle.

2. "The Truth" was the door into the Holy place, the room where they kept the showbread"(the bread of His presence), and the candlestick (the light of His presence).

3. "The Way" was the path through the veil into the Holy of Holies. This was the only way to get into the presence of God. Jesus was talking to the Jews who understood this terminology of these words.

They should have understood that Jesus was saying, that He was the only way into the presence of God. This too, went over their heads, similar to how the parables were. Jesus split the veil in the temple from top to bottom when he died on the cross; signifying that because of what He did, you could now come into the presence of God. The split veil shows that God had been there, but now he was gone. God was alone in the Holy of Holies before the veil split. The Chief Priest was the only one who could approach God by following the prescribed procedures. After Jesus died on the cross, God was approachable again. In Paul's epistles, he used the term "the way" speaking about following Jesus. We need to get in "the Way," and follow Jesus, instead of impeding others and keeping them from following Jesus. Notice in John 14:23, *'Jesus answered and said to him, "If anyone loves Me, he will keep My word; and My Father will love him, and We will come to him and make Our home with him.* Father-God wants to come alive to you. He longs to be your companion and live with you.

We can enter in the presence of Father-God the same way that Jesus does. Father-God wants to have a relationship with you and I. Can you have a relationship without fellowship? How do we fellowship with God? By Fellowship in prayer and reading the Word. When we have a relationship based on our fellowship, we can boldly walk into the presence of Father-God and present to Him our request. Hebrews 4:16, *"Jesus answered and said to him, "If anyone loves Me, he will keep My word; and My Father will love him, and We will come to him and make Our home with him.*

If you say you can't boldly walk into the presence of God, then you don't have a relationship with Him. You CAN have a relationship with Father-God, START TODAY. Pray and read your Bible. Talk to God and then let Him talk back to you. A relationship is a two-way street, talking and listening. Most Christians talk to God but fail to wait and listen to Father-God. By reading the Word, we are reading the thoughts of God. As we read the Word, the Holy Spirit reveals the thoughts of God to us.

## THE PRAYER HABIT

Jesus was a man of prayer and prayer was no duty to Him. It was a glorious privilege. He loved to get up early to pray or pray most of the night like He did the night Peter walked on the water with Him. Remember, that Jesus was living a human life. I am convinced; Jesus did everything he did as a human. He did not draw from His Godly rank any time. I believe that we can do everything that Jesus did here on earth if we did everything He did here on this earth, beginning with His prayer habit. If our prayer habit was the same as His, we could do everything He did in His three-year ministry. Jesus knew what belonged to Him, and

He used His rights. He was still living under the "Old Covenant." He didn't have the benefit of the "New Covenant," a new and better covenant. Most Christians do not know what belongs to them and they do not use their God-given rights. When Jesus cast out demons, He used the authority He has given to the church today. The forces of Hell could not harm or touch Jesus, and He used the same ability he gave to us. The Body of Christ can freely walk in the same life, power, and divine liberty as Jesus walked in by understanding their privileges. This is not extreme teaching; it is walking in the life and authority given to us as Children of God.

We are translated out of the realm of darkness, weakness, and ignorance, into the Kingdom of God. We have been translated into the Kingdom of the Son, Jesus. His love is the realm of wealth, life, light, joy, peace, and faith. Every Child of God should walk on this earth exactly how Jesus did. From His Baptism to the infilling of the Holy Spirit, we must learn and know the Holy Spirit in the same sense as He did. Jesus took advantage of the Holy Spirit within Him by giving him access, and we haven't been able to take advantage of the Holy Spirit living within us yet. I prophesy that in the near future we will. I believe that in God's divine time we will soon take our place as victorious overcoming Christians. The hour is coming before the coming of the Lord that the body will arise and walk before God in that fullness. I'm ready, aren't you? Diseases cannot get a hold of us. We will walk in divine health. Demons will run before us. We will be like a great big bunch of Jesus' all over the earth. We will do the things that Jesus does as if He was there. Jesus made it a habit to talk with the Father. He was so much in tune with the Father, that He said, "I only do what I see my Father do."

How do you make something a habit? By doing it over and over again. Prayer is something you will have to make your flesh surrender to. If you will allow the flesh to be quiet, so you can talk and hear the Father, then you can do the works Jesus did and greater works than He did. Force yourself into a prayer life. Regardless of how you feel, drive yourself into prayer. Your first attempt may halt, stumble and be short. Today, pledge to God, "This week, I will pray 15 minutes each day, and next week increase the time by 15 minutes. The next week, pray for 15 minutes more. Then the fourth week say to yourself, "I will pray for 1 hour." If you pray for one hour a day, you will be an excellent, powerful, and influential Christian. You will see miracles happen when you pray. After the fourth week of prayer, you will suitably be in the habit of prayer. Prayer brings you into personal fellowship and in touch with the Father, the Holy Spirit, and Jesus. All three are brought into your prayer life. You are praying to the Father. You are praying in the Spirit, and you ask it in Jesus' name.

Your prayers are based on the Word of God, which is Jesus. You cannot spend extended time in prayer, without it affecting you. One cannot spend an hour in conscious communion with the Father, Son, and Holy Spirit, on a daily schedule, without the heavenly fragrance of the Father, Son, and Holy Spirit getting on you. It is a sweet fragrance. I smelled it several times when I was in fellowship with God in the Word. Sometimes, my Bible has a sweet fragrance coming out of it; anyone can smell it. It happens every time; I get a revelation from God while reading my Word. When you spend that time in prayer, and the fragrance gets on you, you will be slow to speak, slow to judge, quick to love and quick to help. There will be a holy calmness about you and your life. When you spend that much time in God's presence in prayer, you will partake in their stability. You will find that you have new strengths and steadiness that will make you a blessing to this world.

You can't spend the hour a day with the God of faith, and His love without it rubbing off on you. He will tune you up, charge up your batteries, and adjust your carburetor. This prayer life makes your mountains, and difficulties take their exact position. Want to be a supercharged Christian? Create in yourself a prayer habit. Remember Father-God loves you and is interested in all your problems, big or small. Pray without ceasing, and God will hear and answer all your prayers. Now, your weapon of prayer is getting stronger as you march off to do spiritual battles and be that overcoming, victorious Christian, Christ planned for you to be.

CHAPTER FIVE

# ALL KINDS OF PRAYER

Ephesians 6:18, a ministry failure is a prayer failure. Prayer gives ministry success. Prayer makes your Christian walk a success. I heard my wife Dorothy say this constantly and it is very true, "Much prayer, much power, little prayer, little power." This holds true in our Christian walk. "Much prayer, much success, little prayer no success." Prayer alone is our key to success. Most Christians don't know there are different kinds of prayer.

1. The Prayer of Binding and Loosing
2. The Prayer of Agreement
3. The Prayer of Faith
4. The Prayer of Praise and Worship
5. The Prayer of Commitment
6. The Prayer in Tongues

7. The Prayer of Intercession
8. The Prayer of Petition

We want to talk about "each of these" in more detail, so, let's begin in reverse order.

## THE PRAYER OF PETITION

This is the most common prayer. It is the prayer we pray when we want something from God. For some people, this is the only type of prayer they know about. Matthew 7:7 is a good example of a petition prayer.

*"Ask, and it will be given to you; seek, and you will find; knock, and it will be opened to you. [8] For everyone who asks receive, and he who seeks finds, and to him who knocks it will be opened. [9] Or what man is there among you who, if his son asks for bread, will give him a stone? [10] Or if he asks for a fish, will he give him a serpent? [11] If you then, being evil, know how to give good gifts to your children, how much more will your Father who is in heaven give good things to those who ask Him!"*

## THE PRAYER OF INTERCESSION

The prayer of intercession is a prayer for others, not for yourself. Our nation and those in authority over us, and our Church and Church members need this type of prayer desperately. Romans 8:34b, *"who is even at the right hand of God, who also makes intercession for us."* Jesus is making intercession *FOR* each of us at this very minute. Romans 8:26, *"Likewise the Spirit also helps in our weaknesses. For we do not know what we should pray for as we ought, but the Spirit Himself makes intercession for us with groanings which cannot be uttered.* The Holy Spirit make intercession through us if we allow him. Ephesians 6:18, *praying always with all prayer and supplication in the Spirit, being watchful to this end with all perseverance and supplication for all the saints—* We also need to pray the prayer of intercession. We pray this type of prayer two ways.

1st Corinthians 14:15, *"What is the conclusion then? I will pray with the spirit, and I will also pray with the understanding. I will sing with the spirit, and I will also sing with the understanding."* What is praying in the Spirit? It is praying in your private prayer language, praying in tongues. There is a good purpose for praying the prayer of intercession. 1st Timothy 2:1-2, *"So we might live a quiet and peaceable life."*

## PRAYING IN TONGUES

God knew that this subject was going to give man reasoning problems. Can you find any other topic in the Bible that God uses a whole chapter to explain? How about Faith, prayer, tithing, salvation? No other subject gets so much attention as tongues. The 14th Chapter of 1st Corinthians talks about tongues, a little about prophecy and interpretation, but mostly about tongues. Praying in tongues is very important to you; because it is a type of prayer that Satan can't understand, so he can't set up barricades against the answer.

In Daniel 10:12, we see that Daniel had prayed and did not receive an answer for 21 days. *Then he said to me, "Do not fear, Daniel, for from the first day that you set your heart to understand and to humble yourself before your God, your words were heard; and I have come because of your words. 13 But the prince of the kingdom of Persia withstood me twenty-one days; and behold, Michael, one of the chief princes, came to help me, for I had been left alone there with the kings of Persia.* We see here that Daniel prayed and God heard him and sent the answer as soon as He heard the prayer. The Prince of Persia, the demoniac prince, kept the answer from coming to Daniel and God's angel had to get help from Michael the archangel to get the response to Daniel. When we pray in our English language, the devil can set up roadblocks to keep our answer from getting to us for a while. Praying in our prayer language, the devil can't understand it and can't set up roadblocks to keep our answer from getting to us.

We talk about this in another chapter in this book where we compared it with the Navajos "code talkers" in World War II. If we pray in Spanish, English or French, the devil understands what we are praying for and will try to delay the answer from getting to us; he wants us to stop waiting in faith for the answer. In the Book of Daniel, we see that Daniel had to wait 21 days for his response because the devil had put up barricades to slow his answer. God had sent the solution the day Daniel prayed. We see that praying in tongues confuses the devil, and we can get our prayers answered in a timely matter.

## THE PRAYER OF COMMITMENT

The prayer of commitment is prayed by committing everything to God.

Psalms 37:5, *"Commit your way to the Lord, Trust also in Him, And He shall bring it to pass."* 1st Peter 5:7, *"casting all your care upon Him, for He cares for you."* You cast your cares over on the Lord in the prayer of commitment. In other words, you pray to God and say you cast your cares over to Him then leave them there. There are some things you don't have to pray. How about worries, anxieties, and concerns? Do you need to pray for them? Not if we have already prayed the prayer of commitment.

Matthew 6:25-27, *"Therefore I say to you, do not worry about your life, what you will eat or what you will drink; nor about your body, what you will put on. Is not life more than food and the body more than clothing? 26 Look at the birds of the air, for they neither sow nor reap nor gather into barns; yet your heavenly Father feeds them."*

*Are you not of more value than they?* Jesus is saying in this scripture. Place your cares, anxieties, and worries on me. Your worrying does not change anything. Philippians 4:6 says the same thing. As long as you fret, worry or continue to be anxious about something you have prayed about, you are nullifying your prayers. You have taken back your problems. The prayer of commitment says, to believe His Word. Then you commit your concerns to Him, and you don't have a problem anymore. God has it under control.

## THE PRAYER OF PRAISE AND WORSHIP

This type of praying cannot be done in just a few minutes. We come to minister to the Lord and tell Him how much we love Him. Just worship Him. We are praising God when we show others how good God has been to us. We call it giving our testimonies. Worship is thanking Him for His goodness and mercy. This type of service is for those Christians that are hungry for the presence of God. You don't want anyone there who doesn't want to be there or wish they were doing something else. This type of prayer, you do not petition God for anything. If a person does not want to be in the service and pray the prayer of worship, it is better if they had stayed at home, rather than hindering everyone else. If you impede the rest of the people in the service, you are cursed and not blessed even if you are a Christian, and best if you do not attend. I want you to look at these scriptures and see the secrets of the early church.

Luke 24:50-53, *"And He led them out as far as Bethany, and He lifted up His hands and blessed them. 51 Now it came to pass, while He blessed them, that He was parted from them and carried up into heaven. 52 And they worshiped Him, and returned to Jerusalem with great joy, 53 and were continually in the temple praising and blessing God. Amen."* Acts 2:46-47, *"So continuing daily with one accord in the temple, and breaking bread from house to house, they ate their food with gladness and simplicity of heart, 47 praising God and having favor with all the people. And the Lord added to the church daily those who were being saved."* Notice in these verses the phrase "Praising God" Acts 5:42, *"And daily in the temple, and in every house, they did not cease teaching and preaching Jesus as the Christ."* Notice another word, "Daily"

How often did the early church meet and pray the prayer of Worship and Praise? The early church made it a habit of praying the prayer of Praise and Worship.

How often did they pray this prayer? How powerful is the prayer of Praise and Worship? Read Acts 16:20-25. What type of prayer are Paul and Silas praying? "Please help us out of this mess prayer?" or how about the "You don't love us anymore prayer?" No! They prayed and sang praises, and the other prisoners heard them. It wasn't a silent prayer, was it? Let's check out this next one in the Old Testament. Look in 2nd Chronicle 20th chapter. Jehoshaphat, King of Judah, had three armies coming to capture Judah. Jehoshaphat did not have the manpower to fight against so large an army. What did he do?

Look in *verse 5*. *"Then Jehoshaphat stood in the assembly of Judah and Jerusalem, in the house of the Lord, before the new court."* He called a prayer meeting. The Lord instructed them to go to battle against this vast army. Whose battle was it? Israel's? The King's? No, it was the Lord's battle. If it was the Lord's battle, did Jehoshaphat crawl up on the walls to watch? What did he do? *Verse 17. You will not need to fight in this battle. Position yourselves, stand still and see the salvation of the Lord, who is with you, O Judah and Jerusalem!' Do not fear or be dismayed; tomorrow go out against them, for the Lord is with you."*

What happened next? *Verse 18. And Jehoshaphat bowed his head with his face to the ground, and all Judah and the inhabitants of Jerusalem bowed before the Lord, worshiping the Lord.* They Prayed the Prayer of Praise and Worship. Now, look at *verse 21. And when he had consulted with the people, he appointed those who should sing to the Lord, and who should praise the beauty of holiness, as they went out before the army and were saying: "Praise the Lord, For His mercy endures forever."* What is happening in this verse? What was their praise? Praise the Lord for His mercy endures forever. I would have thought it might have been, "Please, please, please help us!" That is the way we pray sometimes. "Everybody is against me; nobody likes me; why does everything happen to me!"

When they praised and worshiped God, the prayer of worship, what happened? *Verse 22, "Now when they began to sing and to praise, the Lord set ambushes against the people of Ammon, Moab, and Mount Seir, who had come against Judah; and they were defeated."* The Bible teaches that God inhabits the praises of His people. When you start praising God, guess who is coming on the scene? God will show up, and when

God shows up, your deliverance will also happen. When God is on the scene, signs, wonders, and miracles begin. When God is on the stage, people's lives change, people get saved, and people get delivered from the curses put on them. People get healed when God is in the house. I am a firm believer in all praise and worship services. I'm tired of just having "church," singing the same old songs, preaching to the best of our ability and having nothing happen in church, besides getting a little emotional and happy. Then going back home the same way we came to church; nothing has changed. If we don't have God in the House, we are just going thru the motions. The devil is laughing at us because he knows he can have his way with us another week.

## THE PRAYER OF FAITH

Matthew 21:21-22 is an example of the prayer of Faith. *"So Jesus answered and said to them, "Assuredly, I say to you, if you have faith and do not doubt, you will not only do what was done to the fig tree but also if you say to this mountain, 'Be removed and be cast into the sea,' it will be done. 22 And whatever things you ask in prayer, believing, you will receive."* Mark 11:23 says almost the same thing. *"For assuredly, I say to you, whoever says to this mountain, 'Be removed and be cast into the sea,' and does not doubt in his heart, but believes that those things he says will be done, he will have whatever he says. 24 Therefore I say to you, whatever things you ask when you pray, believe that you receive them, and you will have them."* Notice the rules of this type of prayer. It is primarily an individual situation, it is your desire, and it is you praying, not anyone praying with you.

There is no one praying in agreement with you. A lot of the times you are the only one that knows that you are praying the prayer of Faith. When you pray, you believe that you have received it, you will have it. Jesus said that you would. Sometimes we want to apply the rules to other types of prayers to the prayer we are praying. This won't work; it would be like applying the rules for basketball to football. It would mess up the game. It is the same with prayer rules. What if Jesus used the word "if" when He was raising Lazarus from the dead? Lazarus, come forth IF it is thy will or the Lord's. In the prayer of Faith, you don't end your prayer with "if it is thy will." In a prayer of dedication, you do end the prayer with "if it is thy will." You are telling God you are available, and you only want His will in the matter. Like Jesus did in the Garden, before the crucifixion. He said, never the less if it is your will, I will do it. When Jesus prayed for Lazarus, He prayed, I thank you that you always hear me. Jesus used the right rule for this type of prayer, and it worked.

## THE PRAYER OF AGREEMENT

Matthew 18:19, *"Again I say to you that if two of you agree on earth concerning anything that they ask, it will be done for them by My Father in heaven."* Don't put any limitations on this scripture, it will do exactly what it says it will do. Notice the word Will, means it will happen, Look at another scripture. John 14:14 *"If you ask anything in My name, I will do it."* These scriptures don't have any maybe in them. The Greek rendering of this scripture says this scripture this way, "If you ask anything in my name and I don't have it, then I will make it for you." Awesome! You and I can agree on anything, and it is done for us. You and the Holy Spirit can come into agreement on the Word as well. When you are in agreement with the Holy Spirit, it will inevitably happen.

God did not put all the promises, and all the faith statements to fill up space in the Bible. They are there for our benefit. They are for us to use.

Isaiah 43:25-26,

"I, even I, am He who blots out your transgressions for My own sake; And I will not remember your sins. 26 Put Me in remembrance; Let us contend together; State your case, that you may be acquitted. In that scripture notice the words, *"let us contend together,"* this is the prayer of agreement. When we plead together using God's words, it will be mighty and compelling. He says put me in remembrance. Pray His words back to Him or come into agreement with Him and His Words. This is a powerful way to pray.

## THE PRAYER OF BINDING AND LOOSING

Matthew 18:18, *Assuredly, I say to you, whatever you bind on earth will be bound in heaven, and whatever you loose on earth will be loosed in heaven.* There is so much power in this type of prayer, and this could be called a prayer of agreement as well. What you bind on earth will be bound in heaven. God gets into a deal with you. What you loose on earth will be loosed in heaven. Whatever you bind on earth, be sure you "loose" God's answer, or you will have a big mess. What I guess I could say is; bind up the devil's work and loose God's response to those works.

Now that you now know the different types of prayers, you can apply the correct weapon for the situation you are facing and can defeat the devil. Prayer is a mighty weapon when used properly.

## PRAYER AND MIRACLES

If we deny that miracles are for this age, we reject the need and privileges and the benefits of prayer. Prayer has a two-fold benefit. The first is direct fellowship with the Father. The second benefit is the answered prayer that comes to us. Look at what Jesus told the man he healed at the Pool of Bethesda, 1st John 5:14-15 *says, Afterward, Jesus found him in the temple, and said to him, "See, you have been made well. Sin no more, lest a worse thing come upon you." 15 The man departed and told the Jews that it was Jesus who had made him well.* For God to hear our prayer is a miracle, as well for Him to answer it. That is a miracle in itself. Regardless if our prayer is for a postage stamp or a million dollars; it is a double miracle when we receive what we prayed. Any answer that comes by faith is a miracle. If we pray and God changes nature to get our answer to us, that is a miracle! What does God respond to? Our faith! Prayer should be faith in action. Some people pray prayers that are begging and wishing. God doesn't hear wishing and begging. Only faith moves God. *"Without faith it is impossible to please God."* Hebrews 11:6,. God is a FAITH God. We are all born by faith. We have to live by faith. If there are no miracles, then there is no reason for Faith. If there are no miracles, God can't answer our prayers without it being a miracle. The men and women that say God's Word is without error and then in the same breath, say the day of miracles is over; have to be the most mis-led group of people the devil has ever deceived. If we pray at all, we expect our prayers to be heard and then answered. If we pray, we must believe in miracles. Religions that don't believe in miracles are only going through the motions of prayer. They don't expect an answer and don't get one.

In most cases, they are wishing and begging. I believe in prayer. I believe in miracles. I believe in divine intervention. I believe that the prayer in faith reaches Our Father-God, and when it reaches Him, He responds to that faith. Faith causes a person to act like God. Faith speaks about things as though they are. God spoke the world, light, and the universe into being before they were. God was operating His Faith.

## PRAYER, AN EXCURSION INTO THE SUPERNATURAL

When you pray, you are taking an excursion into the supernatural realm. You are going into the Throne Room and in the presence of Father-God. He has promised to hear your prayer and give you your request. You have entered on the grounds of His Word, or you bring Jesus' promise to God, which says, *"Whatsoever you ask the Father in my name, He will give it to you."* Jesus only spoke what He heard His Father speak. Now you come to Father-God in prayer, with Jesus' Words and Father-God's Words, and you appeal to His own Words. Prayer is one of the greatest weapons of offense when applied correctly.

CHAPTER SIX

# THE THIRD WEAPON

## "THE NAME OF JESUS"

The Bible says everything that is named must bow to the name of Jesus. Is Cancer a name? It must bow to the name of Jesus. Is Flu a name? Is depression a name? It must bow to the Name of Jesus.

In Deliverance, we always ask the demon, "what is your name?" We know that his name must bow to the Name of Jesus; so, we say, "In the Name of Jesus come out."

In war, you have to keep your battle plans a secret, so the enemy can't make plans to cause your defeat.

Mark 16:17, *And these signs will follow those who believe: "In My name they will cast out demons; they will speak with new tongues; they will take up serpents; and if they drink anything deadly, it will by no means hurt them; they will lay hands on the sick, and they will recover."* Jesus is saying here in this scripture, "In my name, you will do everything I list here." What does His name mean to the Father, to the church, and to Satan? To the Father, first, Jesus inherited a more excellent name than any of the angels as the First Begotten Son. Second, the Father gave Jesus a name above every name that at the name of Jesus every knee should bow in all three worlds; Heaven, earth, and under the earth or Hell, by His conquest over sin, Satan, disease, Hell, and the grave. He acquired a Name that is above all names. Then, Jesus gave us the legal right to use this name. The Father knew that Jesus' name held unlimited power, and it was His joy to recognize that name when used by those of us that believed and had faith in the name.

The church for years and years has believed in the person of Jesus. That is good, but it is just as important for Believers to believe in the NAME of Jesus, for it is in the NAME that we have His authority. It is in the belief and faith of the NAME that we do everything in Mark 16:15-20 (* added by the author to enhance your understanding although it is implied in the scriptures),

*And He said to them, "Go into all the world and preach the gospel to every creature. 16 He who believes and is baptized will be saved, but he who does not believe will be condemned. 17 And these signs will follow those who believe: In My name they will cast out demons; \* In my name, they will speak with new tongues; 18 \* in my name, they will take up serpents; and \* In my name, if they drink anything deadly, it will by no means by no means hurt them; \* in my name, they will lay hands on the sick, and they will recover."* It is almost beyond our understanding of all the possibilities in using His Name.

There are 336 times in the New Testament, that the phrase "in Jesus Name," and "in my Name" is used. We must have faith "in the Name" to get it to work for us. To have faith in Jesus is wonderful, but if we are going to have miracles happening in our churches, we are going to have to have Faith in the 'NAME of Jesus'. We must have Faith, that when we speak the "NAME of Jesus" something supernatural happens. WE MUST HAVE FAITH IN THE NAME! To the church, when He said *"Whatever you shall ask of the Father in My Name,"* He is giving us a signed check on the resources of heaven and is asking us to fill in the amount we want.

To Satan, it is a Name that makes him shake and tremble when he hears it. It was Jesus who went to Hell to pay for our sins, and then beat Satan to a pulp. In Colossians 2:15, *having disarmed principalities and powers, He made a public spectacle triumphing over them in it.* It says Jesus made a show of Satan and the demons. Jesus dragged them through the streets of Hell, displaying how bad He beat them. One translation of the Bible says "He paralyzed Satan." According to Romans 16:20, *And the God of peace will crush Satan under your feet shortly.*

Jesus then placed Satan under our feet. "Under our Feet" is another expression that most of the believers don't understand. When something was put under your feet in Jesus time, it meant you were totally in control of it. If it was a person, they had to do everything the person whose feet they were under told them to do. The person is in total control of them. Who is under our feet? Why do we let him out from under our feet? We have been given the NAME of Jesus. Put Satan where he belongs and keep him there. Why do we let Satan bother us? Jesus said in the last chapter of Matthew, *"All authority has been given unto Me in heaven and in earth."* Jesus now stands as total master and ruler of the universe. Now we can see why every name must bow to the Name of Jesus.

Most Christians have trouble believing any of this. They have not been taught to believe and have faith in the Name of Jesus. That is why they are always walking around defeated. All, of Jesus, was in heaven, all He won through His death on the cross, and His defeating Satan in Hell; He gave to us! His NAME is all. He was, all He is today, and He gave us His NAME to use. Have you noticed when the police step out into the road with their hand out, everyone stops for them? That little female police officer has the same power as those great prominent male police officers. I still believe those big 18-wheeler trucks are stronger than the police are, and they could keep on driving. Don't you? Why do they stop? It is because the authority of the Name of State has been given to the Police. All the power of the Name of the State would come against anyone who did not stop at their command. When the little policewoman holds her hand up for you to stop; you stop. She can't stop you, but the authority of the Name of the State stops you.

We as Christians must have faith in the power of the Name of Jesus, which has been given to us to use. Why did Jesus give us His name to us? He gave us His NAME that we might carry out God the Father's will here on earth, just like Jesus did when He was here on earth. He gave us the authority to maintain His victory over Satan. People should be talking about us like they did the early Christians in Acts 17:6, *But when they did not find them, they dragged Jason and some of the brethren unto the rulers of the city, crying out, these that have turned the world upside down have come here too.*

## GOD'S PROMISES IN THE USE OF HIS NAME

Let us read some promises. John 14:13-14, *And whatever you ask in My name, that I will do, that the Father may be glorified in the Son. 14 If you ask anything in My name, I will do it.*

Does verse 13 say we can ask for whatever? What is whatever? What does that mean? This scripture means we can ask whatever is the will of God and Jesus said that it will happen. Look at the 14th verse. *You may ask me for Anything in my Name and I will do it.* This scripture says we can ask anything. What is anything? What did Jesus say about it? John 15:16, *You did not choose Me, but I chose you and appointed you that you should go and bear fruit and that your fruit should remain, that whatever you ask the Father in My name He may give you.* How would you explain this scripture? Let us look at a couple more. John 16:23-24, *"And in that day you will ask Me nothing. Most assuredly, I say to you, whatever you ask the Father in My name He will give you. 24 Until now you have asked nothing in My name. Ask, and you will receive, that your joy may be full.*

Jesus had been with these disciples for three years and had been their total support. He was soon going to heaven, and He wanted them to know that He was still going to take care of them. Today Jesus is telling us the same thing. He is going to take care of us. He is giving us the authority to use His NAME. We can ask anything in His NAME and expect to get it. We have His promise of "any and everything." It is ours when we have Faith in His NAME.

## OUR MIGHTY VICTORIOUS SAVIOR

Jesus foretold what he would do when He went to Hell to pay for our sin. Luke 11:21, says, *But when a stronger than he comes upon him and overcomes him, he takes from him all his armor in which he trusted, and divides his spoils.* All the Old Testament saints went to

Abraham's bosom in the inner-part of the earth. Luke 16:19-31, The Bible calls it Hades, Sheol, or Hell. Acts 2:25-35, Jesus went to Hell so you and I could go to heaven. In *Verse 31, he is foreseeing this, and spoke concerning the resurrection of the Christ that His soul was not left in Hades, nor did His flesh see corruption.* This is what happened in Hell. After Jesus paid all our debts, He cast off all the Demon forces, death, and the grave, our sins, guilt, shame, sickness and poverty, and then He began to whip on Satan. Jesus whipped and defeated Satan so much that he was paralyzed. He couldn't do anything because he was completely beaten to submission.

Jesus then preached to the Old Testament Saints in Abraham's bosom. 1st Peter 3:18-19, *"For Christ also suffered once for sins, the just for the unjust, that He might bring us to God, being put to death in the flesh but made alive by the Spirit, 19 by whom also He went and preached to the spirits in prison,"* Ephesians 4:8-10, *"Wherefore he says, When he ascended up on high, he led captivity captive, and gave gifts to men.*

"He ascended"—what does it mean? He first descended into the lower parts of the earth? *10 He who descended is also the One who ascended far above all the heavens, that He might fill all things.* He had taken away the keys of authority that Satan took from Adam; the keys of death and Hell. Revelation 1:18, *"I am He who lives, and was dead, and behold, I am alive forevermore. Amen. And I have the keys of Hades and of Death."*

Keys are the symbol of authority. Example: If I give my keys to someone for the truck, the house, and for them to take care of my things; they have the authority to use them. Jesus also had the very armor in which Satan trusted, just like the first scripture said. Jesus had defeated all the enemies of man, in heaven, earth, and Hell. He now had ALL the authority. He had all the keys of authority God had given Adam before Adam had given them to Satan. Jesus told His disciples in Matthew 28:18, *"All authority has been given to me in heaven and earth."* Jesus now stands as Master, Ruler of the Universe and absolute Victor. His name is above every name because of His mighty conquest, and because He defeated death and Hell, He was given a name that was above every name, and He gave that NAME to us. His authority was given to us that is in the NAME of JESUS.

We now have the authority to use His name. All He was is in that name. All He is today is in that name, and He has given that name to us. "The Name above All Names" was reserved in heaven from the beginning of time, and no one had done anything to deserve it before. Jesus was given that name so that He could give it to us. The reason He gave us the Name was, so we could carry out the Father's will in this time of history that we now live. We know that the early church utilized this authority. They had miracles everywhere they went. The miracles and wonders opened the doors to preach the gospel, which caused thousands to get saved. Two years after the death of Jesus, ninety percent of the known world was reached with the gospel of Jesus. They did all of that by believing in the power of the NAME and using the authority given to them by Jesus.

## AUTHORITY OF THE BELIEVER

A lot of men have religious credentials, but they don't live and walk in the realm of the supernatural. The signs and wonders are what testify of our authority and credentials. Every once in a while, some of us have experienced the authority invested in the NAME of

Jesus. We have seen the miracles of the Bible in our ministry. We have seen the lame walk, the blind see, and the deaf hear, but none of us have been able to make it have a permanent place in our lives; a place where the power of His NAME was in our ministry every day. I long for the time that is coming when the church will stand up and take her rightful authority and reach the world with the Gospel and with the NAME of Jesus, signs, and wonders will be everyday happenings. In that supernatural realm, living as a believer will be very easy, because everything that would come against us, would have to bow to the NAME of Jesus. We would have the same confidence in the Name, as we have in the money that we have in our pockets today.

When are you going to be what Jesus authorized you to be? When are you going to start having faith in the NAME of JESUS and use it to accomplish the will of the Father in this time of history? Jesus ordained every Christian to be a little Jesus with the authority to use that name above every name. The name of Jesus is the name that will heal cancer. The name of Jesus will heal diabetes and high blood pressure. Everything that has a name will have to bow to the name of Jesus. When are you going to become a supernatural Christian like the first church? God is waiting for someone to be bold enough and that believes in the authority of The Name of Jesus, to step up and start commanding those things that are named to be healed.

## THE USE OF THE NAME

The Name of Jesus can't be separated from salvation. The very name is filled with music to repentant believers. Everyone, speak His Name out loud, say "JESUS," again, "JESUS," one more time, "JESUS." There is something wonderful that happens in your heart when you speak His name. Say that Name again, JESUS! Acts 4:12, *"Nor is there salvation in any other, for there is no other name under heaven given among men by which we must be saved."* Not only are we saved in the Name of Jesus, but Matthew 28:19, says this. *"Baptizing them into the NAME of the Father, the Son and the Holy Spirit,"* This scripture says we are not only to be saved by the NAME, but we are also supposed to be baptized into the NAME. Look at this next scripture. Acts 2:38, *"Then Peter said to them, "Repent, and let every one of you be baptized in the name of Jesus Christ for the remission of sins; and you shall receive the gift of the Holy Spirit. 39 For the promise is to you and to your children, and to all who are afar off, as many as the Lord our God will call."* In this scripture, not only are we saved "In the NAME," baptized into the NAME, now we benefit from receiving the Gift of the Holy Spirit because of the NAME. Jesus gave us a lot of promises if we used His NAME. If we used His NAME in prayer, we could expect certain things to happen. In the last lesson we looked at some of the promises, but let us now review them. The first word was "Everything." We can ask for everything in the Name of Jesus. The second word was "Anything." If we ask for everything in Jesus NAME, he will give us anything in His NAME.

We must know the power we have in the authority of the NAME of JESUS before we see signs and wonders happening in the church, just as Peter and John spoke to the lame man Acts 3:1-6 they said *"Then Peter said, "Silver and gold I do not have, but what I do have I give you: In the name of Jesus Christ of Nazareth, rise up and walk."* Most Christians don't know what they have, so they live on defeat. How many times have you walked up to someone and told them, "such as I have, I give to you? In the NAME of Jesus rise up!" Or "in the NAME of JESUS be healed or delivered." When was the last time you spoke the NAME of Jesus with authority? That could be the reason we don't see many miracles.

This Jesus is the one that took all the sins of the world on Him, so we could have the benefit of using His NAME. He went to Hell and paid for our sins. He was raised on the third day for our justification. He is at the right hand of the Father today as an intercessor and Mediator for the whole human race. If we believe that we can be saved by the NAME, but do not believe that NAME can heal us, we should throw the whole Bible away and say it is all a lie. IF we can't think that we have prosperity by that NAME, then why can't we believe we can be victorious in every area of our lives? Most of the church members don't believe and understand His Word. If we did, we would look like the first church. The reason that the rest of the world thinks we are hypocrites today is that the Church is living a lie. They confess that all these benefits are theirs, but act like it is not for today. The Church is destroying the integrity of the NAME of Jesus by not having Faith in the NAME. Civilization is very quickly disintegrating. The wave of crime and lawlessness are by-products of our not having faith "In the NAME!"

Our disobedient, disrespectful children, who are so unruly at home and in the Church services, is the by-product of us not having faith in the NAME of Jesus, because we don't mean what we say. We tell our children, don't do that, but we let them do it. We tell ourselves we believe in the Name, but we don't use it. When are we going to act like the first church?

## IN MY NAME YOU SHALL CAST OUT DEMONS

If you own a house, you probably know what all you have in your home. If you own property, you probably know everything about it. In the physical, we are this way, but in the spiritual, we are too lazy to find out what belongs to us. We seem to have trouble understanding what belongs to us. You remember in the Bible, what Jesus told His disciples as he was about to leave them, *"In my Name, you shall cast out demons."* The large part of Jesus' ministry was filled in combat with the unseen host of darkness. One would think as one listened to all the radio and T.V. ministers that the demons had gone out of existence or they had been herded together to where all the poor people live; or they are spending their time will the lower strata of humanity, you know, at the bars and the drug houses.

I have found that the scriptures say a lot about combat with demons. Ephesians 6:12, *"For we do not wrestle against flesh and blood, but against principalities, against powers, against the rulers of the darkness of this age, against spiritual hosts of wickedness in the heavenly places."* Ephesians 3:10, *"to the intent that now the manifold wisdom of God might be made known by the church to the principalities and powers in the heavenly places,"* Colossians 2:15, this was talking about when Jesus had gone to Hell to pay for our sins and what He did. *"Having disarmed principalities and powers, He made a public spectacle of them, triumphing over them in it."*

Most of the time in the church, the Brothers want to serve God better, but they can't. They will try to but never quite make it. Why? These powers and principalities are keeping them from doing God's work. They want to change but they can't. That is when in Jesus' NAME, we should command those demonic power holds, to break off our brothers and sisters. You can break them off yourself if you have total Faith in the NAME. I don't think that very many successful ministries have gotten successful without knowing that the very air around us is filled with hostile forces. They don't know and how to overcome the hostile forces. They are attempting to keep us from fellowshipping with the Father. Have you ever tried to pray for one hour? Everything in the world happens, so you have to take care of it so you can't pray and fellowship with the Father. There are three things we must know to overcome the enemy. First, we must be children of God. Second, we must not have any unconfessed or unforgiven sin in our heart. If we do, the demons will only laugh at us. Third, we must believe in the power of Jesus' NAME and know how to use it. A lot of folks who come up for prayer for sickness and can't seem to receive it, they are candidates for deliverance and then prayer.

IF your life has been defeated and hemmed in by the power of the adversary, rise up in that mighty NAME of Jesus. Hurl back those demonic forces and take your deliverance, and then go and set others free. What does this expression "in Jesus' Name" mean? The expression "in Christ" is used one hundred and thirty times in the New Testament. It shows the believers position, his legal standing, and his place in the family and the purpose or program of God. When the Early Church used His NAME, it meant that they were representing Him. They were acting in His place, and when they prayed in that NAME, it was as though Jesus Himself was praying. They were taking Jesus Christ's place and acting as Christ's representatives.

When we pray in Jesus' NAME, we are taking the place of the absent Jesus, using His NAME, using His authority, to carry out the Father's will here on earth. Those early Christians, they didn't examine what Jesus said to make sure it was God's will. They didn't pray to see if they felt led to do it. They just did what He said and changed the known world. "Whatsoever you ask the Father in my NAME. He will give it to you." is a declaration that is simple enough for anyone to understand. Here before us is the supernatural power that is available to every believer. Will we use it?

## THE MAN AND THE MIRACLES

Jesus! This real NAME has within it "miracle-working power" even today. Jesus was a miracle worker. Jesus' life was a miracle. He lived and walked His entire ministry in the realm of the miraculous. He made miracles common. One of the outstanding miracles is one we fail to see that it was a miracle. On the day of Pentecost, the people in the upper-room, men and women, went boldly to testify in the streets about the wonder of the Name of Jesus. These disciples hid in fear for 50 days from the very same people they were boldly testifying. A stream of miracles flowed from the hands of the disciples. It upset Judaism and shook the Roman government to its foundations.

Look in John 14:12-13, *"And whatever you ask in My name, that I will do, that the Father may be glorified in the Son. 14 If you ask anything in My name, I will do it."* The believers made an amazing discovery. When they used the NAME of Jesus, they had powers as He had when He walked the earth. Those same powers are yours today if you believe in the NAME. The world would be saying the same thing about you. The sick will be healed, the dead will be raised, and demons will be cast out. When will you be what God planned for you to be? When will you start? You are an offspring of the miracle worker. The miracle-working desire is embedded deep in everyone that calls themselves a believer.

## ARE MIRACLES NORMAL?

Christianity began in miracles; it grows by miracles. Every new birth is a miracle; every answer to prayer is a miracle; every victory over temptation is a miracle. When man's reason takes the place of the miraculous, Christianity loses its very life and becomes a dead religion. Dead religion is a religious gathering that tells stories about when God was extraordinary and miraculous. Christianity is not a religion; it's the life of God in man. Man craves a miracle working God today. It is not God's fault; He has given us the tools to see the miracle-working God today.

John 14:14, *If you ask anything in My name, I will do it.* He has given us the NAME of Jesus. When are we going to use it? The answer for the World is the new Birth, the indwelling of the Holy Spirit and the NAME of Jesus. Prayer becomes a miracle-working force in the world. What does God say He would do if you prayed in the NAME of Jesus? The Bible is a record of miracles and divine interventions. It is a history of outbreaks of the supernatural realm into the natural realm. From the very beginning of time miracles have been normal, from Adam and Eve thru the apostles it was miracle after miracle. We see outbreaks of the presence of God and signs and wonders. Some humble common man, hungry for God, will be the driving force of God showing Himself to the Church. Man will finally understand that God is the same yesterday, today and forever. He will realize he can ask anything in the NAME of Jesus and the Father-God will give to him. We crave for the presence of God to invade our old dead religious services; that have no drawing power to cause the people of the world to want to come in and see God. When services have no ability to heal ALL the sick or no power for the infilling of the Holy Spirit, and without miracles to draw the lost in, a very few people will be saved.

All normal men crave the supernatural; they long to see the manifestation of the power of God and to feel His touch on their lives. A man was created by a miracle working God. That miracle element is in man. Man longs to perform miracles and live in the atmosphere of the supernatural. This miracle element in man has made him an inventor, and discoverer. It caused him to experiment until he had conquered chemicals, electricity, atoms, and the air. This miracle element in man has given us the airplane, submarine, space travel, radio, computers, and all the other devices and miraculous medical procedures.

When believers start having faith in the NAME of Jesus, they will live in the realm of the supernatural without effort. No longer will Faith be a struggle and fight, but we will unconsciously live in the realm of God. The spiritual realm should be the believer's normal operational realm, where he is in constant communion with God. This realm to the Believer is where they automatically operate in miraculous, miracle-working faith, expecting the supernatural to happen. It should be as natural as when a person in the natural writes a check for something and expects the bank to pay the bill from their account. He expects it to be good because he knows he has money in the bank. It will be the same with miracles; He will expect them to happen. What are we waiting for?

## DOES IT TAKE FAITH TO USE THE NAME OF JESUS?

There is no place in the Bible, that I can find, where Jesus mentioned faith or belief when He was talking about using His NAME, except in the future tense. Look at Mark 16:17-18; *"And these signs will follow those who believe: In My name they will cast out demons; they will speak with new tongues; 18 they will take up serpents; and if they drink anything deadly, it will by no means hurt them; they will lay hands on the sick, and they will recover."* In this scripture, the word believer is talking about Christians. A better translation of this word would be "my believing ones." It is saying we have the right to use His name. The right to use His NAME is given to bless the Church. It is a right that belongs to every child of God. We have four different rights with the use of His NAME.

1. We are born into the family, and the NAME belongs to the family.

2. We are baptized into the NAME and we are baptized into Christ Himself.

3. Jesus gave His NAME to us, and His power of attorney to use it.

4. We are commissioned as Ambassadors to go and preach His NAME to all Nations.

I can't see any place where we need to have any special faith to use the NAME of Jesus. Each of us has already been given the measure of faith and the NAME is legally ours to use. If I had a thousand dollars in the bank, it would not take any faith to go withdraw it from the bank. If I wanted to withdraw $1100, it would take faith. Some of us have had the unpleasant experience of overdrawing our account here on earth. Jesus has made a deposit of His NAME into our heavenly account. We can't overdraw regardless, of how many withdrawals we make on it.

## JESUS IS IN THAT NAME

All He was, all He did, all He is, and all that He will ever be is in that NAME. He is healing to us now. He satisfied the claims of justice and became our righteousness. He is now our righteousness. He died that we might live eternally. He is our life now. He is our healing. He is our health, and He is our victory. He is our all in all.

## HIS PROGRAM

If we understood His program for today, the Christians that got sick would just be healed the moment that sickness touched them. The Holy Spirit indwells in us for a purpose. One of the reasons for His indwelling is to heal our physical bodies of diseases that are continually attaching themselves to us — tired of being sick? Recognize the fact that the Holy Spirit is healing the diseases that try to overtake our body. It is part of God's program. 1st Peter 2:24, *"who Himself bore our sins in His own body on the tree, that We, having died to sins might live for righteousness—by whose stripes you were healed.*

Isaiah 53:5.

*But He was wounded for our transgressions, He was bruised for our iniquities; The chastisement for our peace was upon Him, And by His stripes we are healed."* If one would think about these scriptures and believe them, we would also know we don't have to be sick. Our sickness died when we died with Christ. We then arose with Christ and were made alive with Him.

## WE ARE ALIVE

We died to our old sins, we died to our old nature, we died to our old diseases, and we rose with Jesus in the fullness of His life. Free from our old sin nature, free from our sins we had committed, and free from our diseases. We know our old life has no right to reign over us because it is dead. We need to know that sickness has no power to reign over us. It IS DEAD TOO! Christ bore our sin and sickness, so we never need to bear them again. NOW, illness hasn't any right to impose itself upon us, and Satan hasn't any reason to impose sickness upon us. We are ALIVE and FREE from the dominion of disease. When ailments attack, we need to treat them the same way as we treat our old sins. Speak to them and tell them to leave in Jesus' NAME. They don't have any right to stay.

## MY LEGAL RIGHTS

When Satan imposes diseases upon me, I have the right to say, "Satan those diseases were laid on the body of Jesus, and you have no right to put them back on me." Your Confession should be, "Those diseases were put away and I am free of disease as the body of Jesus was when He rose from the dead. I am part of the Body of Christ and you cannot put disease back on the Body of Christ. Do you think that Jesus is going to let Satan put sickness on Him? I don't think so! If Satan should attack my body, all I have to do is call my Father's attention to the fact, and the disease must go because I am free. I know that by His stripes I am healed; and if I am healed, I am well, free from disease. Jesus is my resurrection. He is my life, my salvation, my healing, my health, and He is my victory.

He is my ALL in ALL. He is everything to me. Praise God!

## HIS WORDS ARE TRUE

From the very moment, I confess my sins, the Bible tells me, "He is faithful and righteous to forgive me" and when He forgives me, I am forgiven. It is the same way with sickness, the moment I confess that Satan has put a disease upon me, just at that moment; Jesus is faithful and righteous to heal me. Jesus healed my sickness and forgave my sins. Sin and sickness both come from the same source. God's Word cannot fail any more than God Himself could fail.

## THE PLACE CONFESSION HOLDS IN OUR CHRISTIAN WALK

The church has never given this vital subject a place in its teachings as it should, yet the answer to prayer, the use of Jesus Name, and Faith are utterly dependent upon it. Romans 10:9-10, *"that if you confess with your mouth the Lord Jesus and believe in your heart that God has raised Him from the dead, you will be saved. [10] For with the heart one believes unto righteousness, and with the mouth, confession is made unto salvation."* Anything you want from God you can get the same way as you got your salvation. Confession holds the same place in our Faith walk too. Being a Christian is a confession. Our faith is gauged by our confession. We'll never believe beyond our confession. Not only are we to confess our sin, but we are to admit our position in Christ also. Such as, what the Father has done for us in Christ, our legal rights, what the Holy Spirit has done in us through the Word and what He can do through us. When we have two different confessions, we are in danger from Satan. One confession is based on the integrity of the Word, and the other is based on our sense of knowledge, our doubts, and fears. When someone comes up to be prayed for and receives prayer, but before they leave the church, they tell you to keep praying for them for the same problem; they have just called God a liar and stopped all faith involved in the prayer. They don't believe God is taking care of the problem. They wasted everyone's time getting prayer.

All prayers should be based on the Word of God, and when you have prayer and then ask for everyone to keep on praying for that problem, you have just destroyed the prayer. Your confessions must agree with the Word.

## WHAT POWER IS BEHIND THE NAME OF JESUS?

One day a Pastor was preaching on the *Name of Jesus,* his text was John 14:14, *"If ye shall ask anything in my name, I will do it."* A lawyer was sitting in the congregation, and when hearing the pastor's remarks, the lawyer was intrigued by the legal aspect of those words. He interrupted the pastor with this question, "Do you mean to say that Jesus has given human beings His "Power of Attorney" to use His name? The pastor responded, "Sir, you are a lawyer, and I am only a pastor. Let me ask you that question. Did Jesus give us His "Power of Attorney" to use His Name? The lawyer said, "according to the language in this scripture, He did! He did precisely that." Then the pastor asked, "And can you explain just what that "Power of Attorney" actually means?" The lawyer answered, "That depends upon how much there is in back of the Name; how much authority, and how much power, that the Name represents." God is behind that Name. All of the Godhead backs up the Name. God's person, His integrity, His throne, His existence and all that God is, is behind the Name, which He gave to His Son Jesus Christ. Philippians 2:9-11, *Therefore God also has highly exalted Him and given Him the name which is above every name, 10 that at the name of Jesus every knee should bow, of those in heaven, and of those on earth, and of those under the earth, 11 and that every tongue should confess that Jesus Christ is Lord, to the glory of God the Father.* All that Jesus is-- is in His Name. All that God is-- is behind The Name. One of the keys which unlock the secret to the success of the early Christians was the use of the Name of Jesus. Today as then, believers cast out devils in that Name. Miracles happen in the Name. "In the Name," the sick are healed. Those early Christians performed signs and wonders through the Name.

The Book of Acts records the first thirty-three years of Christianity after Jesus had ascended to heaven. It is proof that the same ministry which Jesus began to do and teach in the Gospel was continued after His ascension, as men and women followed His example and used His Name. Mark 16:15-18, *"And he said unto them, "Go into all the world and preach the gospel to every creature. 16 He who believes and is baptized will be saved; but he who does not believe will be condemned. 17 And these signs will follow those who believe: In My name they will cast out demons; they will speak with new tongues; 18 they will take up serpents; and if they drink anything deadly, it will by no means hurt them; they will lay hands on the sick, and they will recover."* Since that day, the ministry of any man or woman, who follows the example of believers in the Book of Acts, has been confirmed by signs and wonders through the power in Jesus Name. How wonderful to know that God wants His same power which was manifested through followers of Jesus Christ to be the same TODAY! It is so exciting to discover the power that is behind the Name of Jesus, and the authority that a believer has, by invoking that Name.

The third chapter of Acts opens with the account of one of the first great miracles they experienced by using the Name of Jesus Christ. The people had left the upper room filled with the Holy Spirit; the same anointing was upon them as it was on Jesus. These people remembered Jesus telling them that if they believed in His Name, the same works Jesus did, they could do. This has never changed! Today, we can do the same works as Jesus and even greater works if we believe in the Name of Jesus. Acts 3:1, *Now Peter and John went up together to the temple at the hour of prayer, the ninth hour. 2 And a certain man lame from his mother's womb was carried, whom they laid daily at the gate of the temple which is called Beautiful, to ask alms from those who entered the temple; 3 who, seeing Peter and John about to go into the temple, asked for alms. 4 And fixing his eyes on him, with John, Peter said, "Look at us." 5 So he gave them his attention, expecting to receive something from them. 6 Then Peter said, "Silver and gold I do not have, but what I do have I give you: In the name of Jesus Christ of Nazareth, rise up and walk." 7 And he took him by the right hand and lifted him up, and immediately his feet and ankle bones received strength. 8 So he, leaping up, stood and walked and entered the temple with them—walking, leaping, and praising God. 9 And all the people saw him walking and praising God. 10 Then they knew that it was he who sat begging alms at the Beautiful Gate of the temple; and they were filled with wonder and amazement at what had happened to him.*

I want you to think with me, how many times did Jesus walk by this man going into the Temple? Every day in His entire ministry and He did not heal this man. How could this happen? Could this have happened today? When are you going to do it? When are you going to believe in the name of Jesus? God's eyes are looking all over the world for someone to put Him in a position to do miracles. Paul preached "If Jesus were dead, He could do no miracles, but since God raised Him from the dead, He is doing the same miracles which He did before you killed Him. He is doing them as we speak in His Name. If He were dead, His Name would have no power. He is alive, His Name has the same power that He had before He was killed."

What is the matter with the church today? They say they believe the Bible and in Jesus, but they don't believe that His Name has the same power as Jesus. If they did, miracles would be ordinary in the Church. God is calling us all to believe in the Name of His Son. The Name of Jesus meant power in the lives of early Christians. It means the same in the lives of Christians Today. That Name on the lips of believers was as like the rod in the hand of Moses. If the Egyptians could have stolen that rod, they would have stripped Moses of his power. The Devil has stripped the belief in the Name of Jesus from the lips of the believers today. Some denominations preach that the power of Jesus' Name ended when the last Apostle died. Also, by having men in the pulpit that were not filled with the Holy Spirit and saying that they believed that God would do whatever He wants to do. They say "you never know what God wants to do," sometimes He does, and sometimes He doesn't." That is the dumbest thing I have ever heard. Jesus took those stripes on His back that we might be healed and His Name has not lost any of its power today. Are you going to allow this in your life and ministry? Christians today have preached of the miracles of God but do not demonstrate power by believing in the power in the Name. I want to rise up and teach a new generation that believes in the power of Jesus' Name.

I'm tired of powerless Gospel, and I am tired of a defeated church. I'm ready for victory and overcoming in Jesus' Name. On the mission field, we would not have had any impact on Central America if we didn't believe in the Name of Jesus and used the name of Jesus to see miracles happen in our ministry. We saw every recorded miracle that was presented in the Bible, happen in our ministry as we used the name of Jesus. We saw created miracles, the blind saw, the deaf heard, the demons fled, the dead rose up, tumors disappeared, and cancer was healed. The Name of

Jesus works for us, just as it did for the disciples. It will work for you as well. Put it to work for you.

## CHAPTER SEVEN

## THE FOURTH WEAPON

## TONGUES

There was a time when I was so hungry for the Word; I spent all my waking hours reading God's Word. The Word became real to me. For the first time in my life, I was getting a revelation of the reality of God's Word. The first revelation I received was about this scripture; Hebrews 13:8, *"Jesus Christ is the same yesterday, today, and forever."* The reality of this scripture was "if He is the same then what He said in His Word was the same and it never changed," even though I had been taught differently. So, one night around 1:00 am in my living room, I ask that Jesus would fill me with His Holy Spirit and He DID. There was one thing I had asked for and it was that I received the Holy Spirit as the Apostles did, so I would know I had the same thing they had. There was no one but Jesus and me, and He baptized me with His Spirit, and with the evidence of speaking in tongues. I had never been in a Spirit-filled Church in my whole life at that time and did not know anything about getting baptized in the Holy Spirit. All I knew, was that God had heard my prayer and I now had the same thing (being baptized in the Holy Spirit) as the disciples had on the day of Pentecost. Now, I was speaking in my mind, Chinese; which changed as I prayed more and more in the Holy Spirit. This experience is a second experience after accepting Jesus Christ as my Savior. All through the New Testament, we read that the Gentiles who were previously saved received the baptism of the Holy Spirit with the evidence of speaking with tongues.

Many Christian don't even believe in tongues and those of us who have been baptized in the Holy Spirit and speaking in tongues, don't see it as a weapon. According to Jude verse 20, I found out by studying the Word of God, that I could build up my faith, by praying in tongues. Jude verse 20-21, says *"But you, beloved, building yourselves up on your most holy faith, praying in the Holy Spirit, 21 keep yourselves in the love of God, looking for the mercy of our Lord Jesus Christ unto eternal life."* The reality of this scripture is the

Bible teaches us that we all have been given "the measure of faith," but according to this scripture, Jude verse 20, we could build up the size of our shield of Faith. If we prayed enough in tongues, we could stand behind our shield and use the Sword of the Spirit, the Word of God and go on the offense. With a small shield of faith, it would stop all the fiery darts of the devil, but we were always on the defense. By praying in tongues, we can be a force to be reckoned with against the devil. So, if the devil has you on the run, you haven't been praying in tongues enough.

Another example of tongues being a weapon: During World War I, the United States used the Choctaw language as "code talkers." After World War I, the Japanese sent students into the United States to learn all the written native languages. In World War II, while we were fighting Japan, the United States needed a code that the Japanese could not break. They came up with using the Navajo's unwritten language; which proves to be a great success. They inserted code talkers with each combat unit. The "code talker" then could talk to other Navajo code talkers to coordinate the plans of action. The Japanese could not break that code. Tongues are our "code talkers" of the spirit world, as the Navajos were in World War II. The enemy could not understand their language, so they didn't know when and where we would come to attack them.

God gave us a language that the enemy cannot break. Notice in Daniel 10: 12-14, *"Then he said to me, Do not fear, Daniel, for from the first day that you set your heart to understanding, and to humble yourself before your God, your words were heard; and I have come because of your words. 13 But the prince of the kingdom of Persia withstood me twenty-one days; and behold, Michael, one of the chief princes, came to help me, for I had been left alone there with the kings of Persia. 14 Now I have come to make you understand what will happen to your people in the latter days, for the vision refers to many days yet to come."*

Had Daniel been Spirit-filled and talked with tongues, He could have spoken to God, and the enemy couldn't put up barricades to stop the answer from coming to Daniel. If you notice in the 12th verse, God sent the angel to answer Daniel the very first day that he prayed, but it took the angel twenty-one days to deliver the answer. You might ask, "Why does the devil do that to our answered prayers?" First, He is trying to steal your faith in "God." He wants us to quit seeking the answer. The Bible tells us that immediately the devil comes to steal the Word. Luke 8:12, *"Those by the wayside are the ones who hear; then the devil comes and takes away the word out of their hearts, lest they should believe and be saved."*

Speaking to God in tongues is the perfect way to get your prayers answered. When you pray in tongues, it is the Holy Spirit praying through your voice, talking to the Father the perfect will of God. You can't pray wrong when you pray in tongues. The devil can't understand your prayer language and therefore is unable to set up barricades to delay your answer.

If you pray in English, French or Spanish, the devil understands you and can cause your answer to be delayed. Tongues are our "code talkers." The enemy does not understand the Holy Spirit talking through our mouths to the Father. When you use your "code talker," Praying in tongues is undoubtedly the best way to pray the perfect prayer to defeat the devil.

## CHAPTER EIGHT

## THE FIFTH WEAPON

## HIGH PRAISE

Repeat after me. "Blessed be the name of the Lord." Again. "Blessed be the name of the Lord." Now say it as you mean it! "Blessed be the Name of the Lord!" Shout it as loud as you can. "Blessed be the Name of the Lord!!!" That is high praise. Let's check out this one in the Old Testament.

Let's look in 2nd Chronicle 5:12-14, *"and the Levites who were the singers, all those of Asaph and Heman and Jeduthun, with their sons and their brethren, stood at the east end of the altar, clothed in white linen, having cymbals, stringed instruments and harps, and with them one hundred and twenty priests sounding with trumpets—* [13] *indeed it came to pass, when the trumpeters and singers were as one, to make one sound to be heard in praising and thanking the Lord, and when they lifted up their voice with the trumpets and cymbals and instruments of music, and praised the Lord, saying,*

**"For He is good, For His mercy endures forever***," that the house, the house of the Lord, was filled with a cloud,* ¹⁴ *so that the priests could not continue ministering because of the cloud; for the glory of the Lord filled the house of God."*

There is more than shouting, playing of the instruments in High Praise. Notice in verse 13, *"It came even to pass, as the trumpeters and singers were as one."* Do you see it? It's the power of unity as one! When the church gets in one accord and is doing and saying the same thing, God will show up. He will not show up if only the worship team is in one accord and not the congregation. They both have to be in one accord and saying the same thing. I have seen revival meetings where the ministry is in one accord, but not the worship team. They looked like they were putting on a performance and were sucking on green persimmons. You would not find any participating in worship or praise. They would call for the congregation to praise but only the leader was demonstrating praise, the rest were tuning their instruments, checking for the next song. Only when we all are in one accord, God will do supernatural things. I want to say something I have already written in this book, but it bears repeating this. When you start praising God, He will show up, and when God shows up, your deliverance will also happen. When God is on the scene, signs, wonders, and miracles begin. When God is on the stage, people's lives change, they get saved and delivered from the curses put on them. People get healed when God is in the house. The church has known about "High Praise" since the beginning of Christianity, but we have let Satan steal it from us. Now let us get back to the elementary fundamentals of our faith utilizing all our weapons and defeat that deceiver by using "High Praise" to bring God back into our churches.

"Blessed be the name of the Lord. For He is good, and His mercies endure forever. My God can do all things. Nothing is impossible for Him."

High praise is a sharp weapon that wipes the enemy out. Try these:

"Praise the Lord; For His mercy endures forever."

"Praise the Lord; He is my refuge and my fortress."

"Praise the Lord; I trust the Lord."

"Praise God; No evil befalls me."

"Praise the Lord; he delivers me."

"Praise the Lord; God honors me."

"Praise the Lord; He is with me in my troubles."

"Praise the Lord; He satisfies me with long life."

High Praises, especially with His Word will work every time. Praise God for the "I will" in Psalms 91. Check it out and see what God will do for his obedient children.

CHAPTER NINE

# THE SIXTH WEAPON

# "A SHOUT OF VICTORY"

The "High Praises" are similar but different from the "Shout of Victory."

When have you had a shout, a "Shout of Victory" that puts fear in the heart of Satan?

Remember when the children of God marched around the City of Jericho. What did they do the last day? They marched around Jericho seven times, and then, they gave a shout, and the walls sunk into the ground, and they just walked into the city.

Look at 1st Thessalonians 4:16,. *"For the Lord, Himself will descend with a shout with the voice of an Archangel and with the trumpet of God."*

The Lord, Jesus uses the shout of victory that paralyzes the enemy.

The "Shout of Victory" is like a bomb going off amid the devil's ranks. It causes confusion in his ranks. It blows a massive hole in his plans for you and the church. Let's bombard the levels of Hell with a shout.

The shout of faith and victory terrifies the devil and his demons. They can't do the things that they were planning to do to you. It interferes and puts a void in their agendas. Let's give a victory shout!

Now shout "Jesus," again, "Jesus!" Now Louder, "Jesus!!" One more time. "Jesus!!!"

## CHAPTER TEN

# THE SEVENTH WEAPON

# PROPHETIC DECREES WHICH ARE DECLARED PUBLICLY

How about prophetic decrees? Are they one of your weapons? Have you ever used a Decree or declaration? We use them regularly without thinking that's what they are. What are the declarations you have been stating over your wife, your husband, your family, this church, people who don't think as you do, and other churches, etc.?

Have you been complaining or grumbling about something or someone's action? Complaining is a negative declaration of a decree. Doesn't your Bible say, "you can have what you say?"

What does "decree" mean? Webster's New World Dictionary says "a decree' is anything that is settled and unchangeable."

What does "declare" mean? To make it clearly known; announce openly. So, it is a prophetic decree which is clearly announced publicly.

When was the first decree made in God's Word? Look in Genesis Chapter 1. Verse 3, *"Then God said, Let there be light"; and there was light."* This is the first mention of a decree being declared. What happens after the declaration? There was light. When we decree God's word, we will get the same results. We are made in God's image; we are a born-again believer, and we can do greater things than Jesus. In the Bible days, only the King or ruler or others in authority were the only ones who could make decrees. Does this exclude us? No! We have been made kings and priests so we can make decrees. God made a decree involving Noah that said that the world as they knew it was coming to an end. Genesis 6:13, *"And God said to Noah, "The end of all flesh has come before Me, for the earth is filled with violence through them; and behold, I will destroy them with the earth."*

In Matthew 21:19-21, Jesus astonished his disciples by decreeing something to a fig tree.

*20 And when the disciples saw it, they marvelled saying, "How did the fig tree wither away so soon?" 21 So Jesus answered and said to them, "Assuredly, I say to you, if you have faith and do not doubt, you will not only do what was done to the fig tree but also if you say to this mountain, 'Be removed and be cast into the sea,' it will be done."*

In verse 21, we received our authority to make decrees. You need to know that you can make decree scripturally. Matthew 21:21 is a scripture and verse authority to decree and make declarations. Prophetic decrees and declarations must line up with the Word of God if we want them to work for us. Remember what I wrote in an earlier chapter, "The greatest weapons of our warfare are the ones we speak with our mouths."

Now, we are going to decree some decrees and make some prophetic declarations. Repeat after me:

I decree /that souls and more souls /will be saved in this church/ in the coming year /than in any time/ in the History of this church./

I decree /that we will have more money/ to give into the ministry /so we as a church/ can do the things God has called us to do. /

I decree /that me, and my family /will have the joy of the Lord/ and do mighty things/ for the Kingdom of God./

I decree/ that me, and my family /will give and it shall be given back to us/ good measure/ pressed down / shaken together /and running over/ shall men give unto us/ because we are givers./

I decree/ that our Pastors will have the mind of Christ /in all matters/ pertaining to the work of the kingdom/ and his vision/ and we will join with them/ to see their vision completed./

I decree/we will walk in Divine Health/ the rest of the year./

I decree/ that there will be signs and wonders /happening weekly in my church./

If you haven't been making decrees based on the Word of God with public declarations you are not using all your weapons to be that overcoming, victorious Christian.

As a way of review:

## THE SEVEN WEAPONS OF OUR WARFARE

1. Sword of the spirit

2. Prayer

3. The name of Jesus

4. Tongues

5. High Praise

6. Shout of victory

7. Prophetic decrees

Use all your weapons to defeat the enemies of your Christian walk and become a victorious, miracle-working, overcoming Christian who makes a difference to their church, town, county, state, and country for the Glory of God.

# ABOUT THE AUTHOR

Dr. T. Jerry Caver got saved when he was nine years old and has always been tender to the things of God, and had a strong desire to share it with those who had not heard.

When he was 25 years old, he got a call from a High School classmate who was working for the Selective Service Administration. She said she was mailing out his "greetings," that he had been drafted. She said if he didn't want to go into the Army, he had better join the branch of service that he wanted. He joined the U.S. Air Force. He spent 5 ½ years in the Air Force, 3 ½ years in Vietnam. He was wounded twice, but he knew God was still in control of his life. He came home and tried to be the best Christian he knew how to be.

Dr. T. Jerry Caver spent his first 30 years of life in a denominational church, where he served God by leading the music, teaching in Sunday school, and the Training Union and working with the young men on Wednesday night. It was from there that he went on his first mission trip to Mexico that changed the course of his life. Afterward, the Holy Spirit gave him such a hunger for the Word of God that he kept reading the Bible. He could not get enough of God or the studying of His Word.

Dr. T. Jerry Caver has taught the Bible for over 60 years. He has spent approximately 50 years of his life in mission work in Central America. It was in this mission field where Dr. T. Jerry Caver saw every miracle that is recorded in the Bible, happen in his ministry. He now resides in Kildare, Texas with his wife, Dorothy, and is available for speaking engagements at your church or event.

# ALL BOOKS BY DR. T. JERRY CAVER

Thank you for reading Weapons of Our Warfare. We hope you enjoyed reading and will tell your friends about it.

Weapons of Our Warfare by Dr. T. Jerry Caver

God has given us the weapons to be that overcoming, victorious church that we read about in the Bible. Learn to use your weapons of this spiritual warfare and you can be more than a conqueror.

Available in Print and Kindle.

Check out Dr. T. Jerry Caver's other books that can be purchased on Amazon.

I Knew a Man by T. Jerry Caver.

This is a true story of a man's triumph and his failures. A story about a man's life that he wants to share with generations to come. This story shares some of the sad and happy times of his life. Read of His beginnings to nearly the end, which hasn't been written

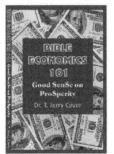

Biblical Economics 101 by Dr. T. Jerry Caver

I was floundering in debt, working three jobs making $3,620.00 a week and could not pay my bills. I was losing my home in one week and then I cried out to God to show me how to get out of debt? That was when He taught me Bible Economics 101.

## FOR MORE INFORMATION

Write to: Dr. T. Jerry Caver

8384 FM 125 South

Bivins, Texas 75555 or


E-mail - glorytogodministry@yahoo.com


Facebook – https://www.facebook.com/tjerryc


Home Phone 903-796-1851

Call for dates available.

Made in the USA
Columbia, SC
06 June 2023

17733065R00081